The impact of tourism on the environment

GENERAL REPORT

ORGANISATION FOR ECONOMIC
CO-OPERATION AND DEVELOPMENT
PARIS 1980

The Organisation for Economic Co-operation and Development (OECD) was set up under a Convention signed in Paris on 14th December 1960, which provides that the OECD shall promote policies designed:
- to achieve the highest sustainable economic growth and employment and a rising standard of living in Member countries, while maintaining financial stability, and thus to contribute to the development of the world economy;
- to contribute to sound economic expansion in Member as well as non-member countries in the process of economic development;
- to contribute to the expansion of world trade on a multilateral, non-discriminatory basis in accordance with international obligations.

The Members of OECD are Australia, Austria, Belgium, Canada, Denmark, Finland, France, the Federal Republic of Germany, Greece, Iceland, Ireland, Italy, Japan, Luxembourg, the Netherlands, New Zealand, Norway, Portugal, Spain, Sweden, Switzerland, Turkey, the United Kingdom and the United States.

CONTENTS

3

PREFACE

The rapid growth of tourism since 1950 has resulted in a degree environmental degradation in a number of OECD countries. These countries have requested that the OECD examines the problem and subsequently the Group of Experts on Environment and Tourism was established in 1977 as part of the Work Programme of the Environment Committee. The Group was asked to analyse the different effects of tourism on the environment and to determine to what extent and by what means these effects could be reduced or prevented. This publication is the final output of the programme of work which was concluded in Salzburg in October 1978 with a Special Session attended by members of the Group and by experts in various fields of tourism and political personalities responsible for tourism and the environment.

The work of this Group was in large part based on two types of reports provided by the Member countries participating in this project:

- the first were national reviews describing the general situation of tourism and the environment, and also government policy in this field including the planning and development measures taken in tourist areas in order to protect the environment;
- the second type consisted of concrete case studies in a number of Member countries analysing the impact of tourism and its economic implications in a given tourist resort. * These studies were designed in particular to throw light on the relationship between variations in income from tourism and changes in the environment;
- in addition, the Secretariat considered special questions relating to tourism and the environment such as the absorptive capacity of tourist areas, measures to reduce the influence of traffic on tourist areas, or the effects of tourism on the economy and the environment.

From the twelve national reviews, the nineteen case studies, from the reports of the Secretariat and the discussion which took place during meetings, the Group was able to draw a series of conclusions and prepare recommendations concerning the environment and tourism.

---

* The case studies are published in a separate volume.

These were adopted by the Environment Committee and then by the OECD Council at the Meeting of Environment Ministers held in Paris on 7th and 8th May, 1979.

The studies and the resulting policy recommendations are to initiate a number of concrete measures in favour of the environment:

i) in the first place, it is expected that the Member countries which supported the launching of the Environment and Tourism Programme, took part in it and approved the conclusions, will apply the recommendations adopted by the OECD Council. It is planned, moreover, that the OECD will monitor the implementation of these recommendations by the different countries;

ii) the Organisation is giving assistance to countries wishing to draw up legislation concerning the environment and tourism or plans for tourism management and development;

iii) the co-operation, which already exists between the various international organisations dealing with questions relating to tourism and the environment, will continue, particularly with regard to establishing tourists' rights and duties, and also formulating environmental guidelines for the development of tourism;

iv) lastly, as part of the Programme of Work of the OECD on the State of the Environment, environmental indicators relating specifically to tourism are to be developed with the objective of assessing any changes in the quality of the environment due to the growth of tourism.

The indications are that tourism will continue to grow, with the result that the pressure on the environment will be still greater. This danger, which is now realized by the majority of governments should prompt them to take measures to ensure both the future of tourism and the preservation of the environment – tourists being the first to benefit from such measures. The objective of this report is to provide guidance in implementing such a policy.

CONCLUSIONS OF THE SPECIAL SESSION OF THE OECD GROUP OF EXPERTS ON ENVIRONMENT AND TOURISM

On the invitation of the Austrian government, the Group of Experts on Environment and Tourism held a special session in Salzburg on 17-20 October, 1978.

In the course of the special session three working groups were set up to discuss in more detail:

i) International co-operation.
ii) Economic and financing aspects.
iii) Standards, regulations and planning.

The working groups prepared a set of conclusions which were adopted by the full session.

A. GENERAL

1. Tourism today is one of the fastest growing sectors and has become an important component in the economic structure of a large number of OECD countries. The number of international travellers in the world has increased from 25 million arrivals in 1945 to 240 million in 1977. * About 70% of international tourist travel takes place in OECD countries. Domestic tourism has also grown at a fast rate.

2. Tourism has generated substantial social and economic benefits. It has made significant contributions, amongst other things, to welfare by increasing and enlarging the alternatives for recreation, created employment as well as becoming for some Member countries the largest foreign exchange earner. International tourist payments in the OECD area have grown from $ US 6 billion in 1960 to more than $ US 40 billion in 1977.

3. Environment is an important input into tourism and therefore the maintenance of a "good" environment is essential to further growth of tourism. Conversely, a degradation of the environment

---

* According to the statistics provided by the World Tourism Organisation.

7

could result, and in certain areas has already brought about a decline in the growth of tourism.   On the other hand in a number of places tourism has helped to improve the environment.

4.   Tourism is to a large extent an activity carried out in the private sectors of the economy and market incentives have contributed significantly to the rapid growth of tourism.   However, the market mechanism alone cannot be expected to ensure that environmental degradation will not take place.

a)   The market takes usually a relatively short-term view, while environmental consequences are characteristically of a long-term nature.

b)   The market cannot measure the changes in the multitude of components that contribute to environmental quality; and the market does not reveal this information, even when it is available.

c)   There are environmental assets which should be preserved despite their potential touristic exploitation; these might be the conservation of valuable ecosystems and landscapes, unique sites, monuments, etc.

5.   It is the responsibility of governments at the appropriate levels, local, national and international, to ensure that the environment is maintained in a condition which corresponds to the needs of the tourists, the local inhabitants and to national objectives. *

6.   For these purposes and based on economic, social and welfare considerations, governments have to apply a large variety of measures: information and education, economic measures including financing of environmental protection, standards and regulatory instruments, planning and management measures.

7.   It is recognized that pollution control and environmental protection are not without cost.   Large sums are at present already raised from the tourists themselves or tourism related establishments, but there is evidence to show that in many tourist receiving regions inadequate funds are being spent on the protection of the environment.

B.   INFORMATION AND EDUCATION

1.   As a first step in the information process it would be necessary to inform tourists, the tourist industry, and local communities of the need and ways and means to preserve and improve the environment, and to influence their behaviour to this effect.

_____

*   The appropriate level of governmental responsibility will vary from country to country.

2.   Useful information could be provided by preparing internationally agreed environmental criteria for the description of tourist areas.   These criteria would in turn facilitate the descriptive listing of tourist receiving regions as regards their environmental quality, for the information of potential tourists.   This descriptive listing could be monitored and readjusted from time to time.

3.   Bearing in mind the need to maintain the quality of the environment and to meet the expectations of tourists, whose behaviour is sometimes detrimental to the environment, it is proposed that OECD Member countries in conjunction with the work of appropriate international organisations draw up a Charter of the rights and obligations of tourists with regard to the preservation of the environment and accordingly set out an action plan with respect to information and education.

C.   ECONOMIC MEASURES AND FINANCING NEEDS

1.   "The Guiding Principles Concerning International Economic Aspects of Environmental Policies" and "The Implementation of the Polluter-Pays Principle" as adopted by OECD Member countries, are also applicable to the implementation of environmental policies concerning tourist activities; the application of these principles will avoid discrimination between tourist receiving areas.

2.   Direct financing of environmental protection by the polluter would result not only in raising funds for such a purpose but also in a reduction of the impact of pollution.

3.   It is generally recognized that direct financing from proceeds of charges on tourists will not provide sufficient funds and that consequently a substantial proportion of funds must come from other budgetary sources.   It is recognized that there is wide variation between countries in their capacity to raise these funds and to share revenues and burdens between various levels of governments.

4.   In countries where the principle of matching financing between central and various levels of local government is accepted, then it is suggested that additional central government finance could be made available to supplement the funds raised by the lower levels of government from the polluter or user.

5.   There is a good case for governmental assistance for environmental protection in tourist receiving regions where tourist development is part of a regional development policy or when tourism is directed towards specific well defined social policy objectives.

6.   At the time of serious short-run economic fluctuations, resulting in a decline of tourist activities or in a transitional period

during the implementation of a major environmental measure, central government finance could be useful to supplement local government funds for environmental purposes.

7. Some countries expressed the wish that OECD allocate the necessary resources for investigating the financing aspects of environmental protection in tourist areas which will make the best use of studies already available.

D. STANDARDS AND REGULATIONS

1. The formulation of environmental standards is the responsibility of the authorities in each Member country. These standards should take into account the environmental expectations of the tourists and might in certain respects need to be more stringent than in non-tourist areas. These more stringent standards should be designed in the light of the financing abilities of the individual regions.

2. The particular areas for which standards should be prepared and for which authorities should develop and enforce mandatory requirements and guidelines are air quality, water quality for drinking and recreation, and soil conservation.

3. Both the tourists and those who offer services and goods to tourists should comply with requirements designed for the protection of the region and respect for cultural traditions. These aims can be achieved by statutory requirements for design and performance standards.

E. MANAGEMENT AND PLANNING

1. Authorities have a role to play both in influencing the demand for environmental facilities as well as their supply in tourist regions:

a) On the demand side the reduction of peak tourist demand over time would reduce the pressure on the environment and such policies, e. g. staggering of school holidays, should be vigourously pursued; these would be particularly effective and cost saving in relation to sewerage, solid waste disposal, noise pollution, building and traffic density control.

b) On the supply side information should be collected for assessing the carrying capacity of tourist receiving areas according to the nature and range of their tourist resources; the physical ecological, social/cultural and psychological aspects of the regions and their population should be taken into account; the emphasis given to each will vary over time and from site to site.

c) Some areas of a particularly sensitive nature will require special protection to severely limit or close them entirely to visitors, with the ultimate protection being provided by state ownership. Some other areas will present a delicate equilibrium between nature, agricultural activities and tourism, e.g. mountain regions and alpine areas, and will require special attention.

2. National authorities should encourage local authorities to ensure that their decisions are based on the fullest available information on the potential environmental impact; when such information is not adequate, it should be sought. Environmental Impact Assessments could be used to evaluate the potential damage to the environment of tourist proposals in the light of forecasted growth and peak demand. Alternative sites for developments should be considered, taking into consideration local constraints and limits to capacity.

3. Depending on the system of government, there is a range of alternatives available as to the allocation of specific responsibilities to various governments levels and several different combinations are in fact in operation in Member countries. To encourage the implementation of central policy at regional and local level, there are also various alternative ways available, from direct enforcement to the provision of incentives or disincentives and the power of persuasion. Irrespective of the system used, it is essential that there be a means whereby local decisions are also harmonized with the achievement of national goals. In general, in the majority of Member countries the following allocation of responsibilities would produce the best path in policy formulation and implementation and might be applied regarding the preservation of the environment.

a) Central Governments should formulate national policies and national tourist plans as linking factors between sectoral plans. Information and guidelines to other levels of government should be provided as well as incentives or disincentives to apply government policy and planning. They should provide a framework for planning at regional and local levels and review, monitor and enforce plans. Regional Governments have a similar role on the regional scale.

b) National Authorities should prepare an inventory on an internationally comparable basis of the following types of areas:
  - sites already developed for tourism with capacity for further development,
  - sites with potential for development as new tourist areas,
  - sites requiring remedial action.

c) From this inventory, and from a policy classification based on the different holding capacity of sites, a planning statement should be prepared defining strategy for locations, and development on one hand, and environmental improvement on the other, and integrating, in this light tourist development with the economic, regional development and social and land use planning.

d) Local Government is the action level where the policy of both central and regional levels is implemented and local land use planning takes place. It is vital that local governments are involved in the formulation of policy and are provided with power to implement these plans.

4. Public Participation in environmental policy formulation is now recognized and used in the majority of Member countries and can usefully be applied to problems associated with tourism. Where such practices are acceptable, Governments should take into account the wide variety of views of their communities either in the form of direct participation in decision-making or of consultation before decisions are taken. Such procedures will improve the understanding of local communities that the long term conservation of tourist assets is a sound economic policy in overall national terms.

RECOMMENDATION OF THE COUNCIL
ON ENVIRONMENT AND TOURISM

(Adopted by the Council at its 490th Meeting on 8th May, 1979)

The Council,

Having regard to Article 5(b) of the Convention on the Organisation for Economic Co-operation and Development of 14th December, 1960;

Considering that tourism constitutes a major economic activity in a number of Member countries and that its further expansion will continue and is desirable both for the economy and for the social well-being of the community;

Considering that tourism can further the creation of employment and regional development;

Considering that environmental resources are a major element of tourism and that a good environment is an essential quality of tourist areas;

Considering that unrestrained growth of tourism could reduce the quality of tourist areas and possibly their income earning capacity;

Considering that tourism plays a major role in the development of international understanding;

Having regard to the Recommendation of the Council of 26th May, 1972, on Guiding Principles Concerning International Economic Aspects of Environmental Policies (C(72)128);

Having regard to the Recommendation of the Council of 14th November, 1974, on the Implementation of the Polluter-Pays Principle (C(74)223);

Having regard to the Recommendation of the Council of 12th October, 1976, on Principles Concerning Coastal Management (C(76)161(Final));

Having regard to the work of intergovernmental organisations concerned with environment and tourism;

On the proposal of the Environment Committee:

1. RECOMMENDS that Member countries fully integrate environmental considerations, at the earliest possible stage, in their tourism development policies and strategies in order to ensure that the development of tourism is in keeping with the conservation of environmental quality.

2. RECOMMENDS that Member countries be guided in the development of their tourism industry by the Guidelines Concerning the International and Economic Aspects of Environmental Policies in Tourist Areas, contained in the Annex to this Recommendation of which it forms an integral part.

3. RECOMMENDS that Member countries co-operating at international level develop a set of appropriate, practicable environmental indicators for tourist receiving areas in order to assist the relevant authorities in developing and implementing tourist policies which will be consistent with environmental needs.

4. RECOMMENDS that Member countries take appropriate steps to ensure that environmental considerations are duly incorporated in any definition of the rights and duties of tourists established at national or international level and are followed by appropriate information and educational campaigns.

5. RECOMMENDS that Member countries take appropriate steps at national and international level to ensure that due account is taken of environmental considerations by competent public authorities as well as tourist organisations and enterprises.

Annex

GUIDELINES CONCERNING THE INTERNATIONAL AND ECONOMIC ASPECTS OF ENVIRONMENTAL POLICIES IN TOURIST AREAS

I. INTERNATIONAL ASPECTS

1.   The "Guiding Principles Concerning International Economic Aspects of Environmental Policies" and "The Implementation of the Polluter-Pays Principle" as adopted by OECD Member countries are also applicable to the implementation of environmental policies concerning tourist activities; the application of these principles will avoid discrimination between tourist receiving areas.

2.   Member countries should co-operate in the preparation of a set of objectives and basic environmental indicators appropriate for the description of the state of the environment for tourist receiving areas.

II. NATIONAL MEASURES

A .   Standards and Related Regulations

1.   In compliance with the Recommendation on "Guiding Principles Concerning International Economic Aspects of Environmental Policies", the formulation of environmental standards is the responsibility of the competent public authorities and takes account of "different social objectives and priorities attached to environmental protection and different degrees of industrialization and population density". The same applies to the formulation of standards in tourist receiving regions to meet the environmental expectations of tourists. In tourist areas standards should be designed in accordance with the health, leisure and relaxation requirements of tourists. These standards will have to take into account the financing abilities of the individual regions.

2.   All aspects of tourism should be brought into line with environmental conditions in the area concerned, e. g. in mountain and coastal regions. Attention should be paid to the preservation of agriculture and forestry in order to harmonize tourism and environmental policies.

3.   Bearing in mind that continued orderly development of the tourist industry depends on the maintenance of the resource on which it is based, the competent authorities should ensure that also those who offer services and amenities to tourists should comply with requirements designed for the protection of the region and respect for cultural traditions.   These aims can be achieved by statutory requirements to ensure high standards for services and amenities and by the accuracy of environmental information supplied to prospective tourists.

B.   Planning and Management Measures

4.   In order to conserve natural, cultural and man-made resources which are the basic qualitative elements of tourism, it is essential that the competent authorities should develop environmental guidelines for tourism development plans, in particular with respect to the quality of air and water (potable and recreational), soil conservation, the protection of natural and cultural heritage and the quality of human settlements.

5.   The competent authorities should ensure that in tourist areas, particular attention be paid in relation to peak demand, to sewerage, solid waste disposal, noise pollution, building and traffic density control.

6.   All possible incentive actions should be taken in the public and private sectors to spread tourism demand over time and hence reduce stresses on the environment; to this end the staggering of holidays and "flexible weekends" should be encouraged.

7.   From the national listing mentioned in paragraph 11 hereunder and from description based on respective carrying capacity of sites, a planning statement should be prepared defining strategy for locations to be developed on the one hand, and environmental improvement on the other, and integrating tourist development with the economic regional development, including social concerns and land use planning.

8.   The competent authorities should ensure that decisions on tourist development plans are based on the fullest available information concerning their environmental implications; when such information is not adequate it should be sought.   Environmental Impact Assessments should be used for major tourist developments to evaluate the potential damage to the environment in the light of forecasted tourism growth and peak demand.   Alternative sites for development should be considered, taking into account local constraints and the limits of environment carrying capacity.   This capacity includes physical, ecological, social, cultural and psychological factors.

9.   Bearing in mind that the carrying capacity will vary from site to site, statutory powers should be used to limit developments in

particularly sensitive areas requiring special protection, which may entail limiting access to these areas with ultimate protection being provided by public ownership.

10.   On the basis of environmental indicators, as mentioned in paragraph I. 2 of these Guidelines, governmental authorities should monitor the state of the environment in major tourist receiving areas and assess the changes in the environmental quality of these areas; the resulting information would be of value to both decision-makers and tourists.

C.   Specific Tasks of Governments

11.   The allocation of responsibility will, in environmental matters, vary from one country to another for constitutional reasons. In general, governmental authorities will need to carry out the following specific tasks related to tourism when formulating policies and programmes concerned with environmental quality and development:

    a)   Identification of the following types of areas:

        i) sites already developed for tourism with capacity for further development;

       ii) sites with potential for development as new tourist areas;

     iii) sites requiring remedial action from the environmental point of view.

        The appropriate set of environmental indicators, as proposed in paragraph I. 2 of these Guidelines, could be used for this identification procedure.

    b)   Development and adoption of environmental quality standards for significant tourist areas, which are consistent with the environmental, social and economic (including tourism) objectives and policies, are the responsibility of the jurisdictions and/or authorities concerned.

    c)   In a number of Member countries the local level of government is the level where the policy of both central and regional levels is implemented and local land use planning takes place. This is the level at which decisions on carrying capacity (see paragraph 8 above) can be enforced by regulation of access. It is essential that there be means whereby local decisions contribute to the achievement of national goals.

D.   Public Information and Participation

12.   While tourists are expected to abide by the law of the country, governments and/or other appropriate bodies are responsible for providing the public with information on how to respect environmentally

sensitive and cultural areas. Such action should be supplemented by the display of posters and distribution of brochures in tourist areas and also by the inclusion in school curricula of appropriate conduct to be observed in areas of cultural and natural importance.

13.   Governments should take into account the variety of views of their communities on the environmental impact of tourism projects, either in the form of practical and appropriate participation in decision-making or of consultation before decisions are taken. Such procedures will improve the understanding of local communities that the long-term conservation of tourist assets is a sound economic policy in overall national terms.

E.   Financial Aspects

14.   Since it is recognized that direct financing from tourist generated revenue may not always be sufficient for environmental purposes, governments may consider granting a proportion of funds provided that the allocation of such funds abides with the Guiding Principles Concerning International Economic Aspects of Environmental Policies and responds to overriding national economic and social requirements, bearing the following considerations in mind:

    i)   government assistance for environmental protection in tourist areas can be justified in view of the social aims of tourism;

    ii) similarly, it is also justified when tourist development is part of a regional development policy.

15.   Proposed plans for the development of tourism, whether at national, regional or local levels, should be subjected to financial and cost-benefit appraisals of their effects on the areas concerned and should include provision for the financing of environmental protection.

ENVIRONMENT AND TOURISM:
THE PRESENT AND THE FUTURE

I

AN OVERVIEW OF THE PRESENT STATE
AND THE FUTURE PROSPECTS *

In a number of OECD countries, tourism is a rapidly expanding industry whose economic advantages are many.

But this fast rate growth (over the past thirty years) has not been achieved without adverse effects on the environment, and there is now some anxiety as to the future of tourism and its increasing cost.

It therefore seems advisable to assess the present situation and consider future trends, so that the growth of tourism can be channelled in ways best suiting both tourism and the environment.

THE PRESENT SITUATION

The two salient features of the present situation are:

- divergences and conflicts between the objectives of tourism and environment;
- the impact of environmental degradation induced by tourism.

A. Divergences between tourism and environmental objectives

This divergence of interest may be explained in the following way:
- on the one hand, a high-quality environment is essential for tourism,
- on the other hand, the quality of the environment is threatened by tourist development itself which is promoted in a certain number of OECD countries because of its economic importance.

a) Requirements for a high-quality environment

i) In surveys carried out in several countries on the factors which determine tourist demand, the tourists themselves have made

---

*   I. Vasallo, Department of Tourism, Madrid, S. Delalande, Paris.

their requirements quite clear. * These surveys also show that, after allowing for the differences between different types of holidays, there are no significant variations in the 'desirability factors', indicated by tourists, irrespective of country or region.

The main deciding factors are the following:
1. attractiveness of the landscape,
2. climate, combined with clean air, clean water and a restful atmosphere,
3. the cost of the holiday,
4. the region's intrinsic qualities (including its gastronomical attractions) and various other factors.

Hence an unpolluted environment of high quality is tourism's raison d'être, and its preservation is in the best interests of all who live by tourism and those for whom it is a form of recreation.

ii)   Nor should it be forgotten that the environment is a "perishable commodity", hard to restore and in short supply, while tourism, the "consumer" of this commodity, instead is a dynamic, fast-growing activity. Increased vigilance will therefore be necessary in order to protect the environment if it is not to become too scarce and damaged a good - one effect of which would be to harm activity.

iii)   Lastly, owing to increasing urbanization and industrialization, the preservation of a certain amount of unpolluted, natural space of high quality appears essential so as to maintain general ecological balance and enable city-dwellers to relax in a healthy natural environment.

b)   Conflicting with these requirements, there are economic objectives which run counter to environmental considerations

The policies of some governments tend to promote the expansion of tourism for the following reasons:

i)   It is a means for developing and rehabilitating regions where incomes are low, where there is no industry and traditional activities are declining, as in mountain areas. Added to tourism's direct effects on the economy are multiplier effects benefiting other sectors indirectly linked with tourism (building).

ii)   Tourism is a considerable source of employment, particularly for unskilled labour and for women.

iii)   For some countries, tourism is a relatively substantial source of foreign exchange which helps to correct the trade balance: in

*   These surveys are listed in the work of J. Krippendorf.

22

1976, the share of international tourism receipts in exports of goods and services was 23.5% for Austria, 21.3% for Spain, 18.5% for Greece and 12.7% for Portugal,* thus indicating the far from negligible role of tourist receipts in certain countries.

Owing to this paradoxical situation, that is, the promotion of tourism combined with preservation of the environment, various problems arise:

- Regions with an environment of high quality, well suited for developing tourism, are faced with the following dilemma:
  - whether to promote such an economic activity, and in so doing accept a certain degree of environmental deterioration;
  - or whether to give priority to environmental conservation, but then forfeit some of the potential income from tourism.

This problem is particularly acute for economically disadvantaged areas where, as is often the case in mountain areas, the quality of the environment is the only resource which can be exploited.

A happy medium must hence be found between "tourist growth" and "environmental conservation", this calling for careful choices which while neither detrimental to one nor the other, will instead promote the tourist industry from a qualitative as well as from quantitative standpoint.

- Conflicts may also arise between those who want to encourage the development of tourism and those who want to restrain it:
  - the former, consisting of that part of the local population which lives by tourism (shopkeepers, contractors, etc.) or of those engaged in the promotion of tourism and who often come from outside (travel agencies, hotel keepers, caterers, etc.) are generally in favour of mass tourism, more profitable for them but more harmful to the environment;
  - the latter, comprising the rest of the resident population (those who "put up" with tourism), certain tourists, and those who claim to militate in favour of nature and the environment, instead oppose the development of any such economic activity and are more concerned with preserving the common natural or cultural heritage.

In fact, two conflicting parties have to be reconcilied: one seeking short-term private advantage, the other upholding the longer-term public interest.

---

* Tourism Policy and International Tourism in OECD Member Countries, 1978, OECD.

B. Impact of tourism on the environment: short and long-term
effects

The environmental damage which tourism or its excesses may
cause can be classified as follows:

a) Effects of pollution

i) Air pollution mainly due to motor traffic and to the
production and use of energy.

ii) Water pollution (sea, lakes, rivers, springs), due to:

- discharge of untreated waste water due to the absence
  or malfunction of sewage treatment plants;
- discharge of solid waste from pleasure boats;
- motor-boating (discharge of hydrocarbons).

iii) Pollution of sites by littering (picnics, etc.) and the
absence or inadequacy of waste disposal facilities (mainly household
waste).

iv) Noise pollution, due mainly to motor traffic or the use
of certain vehicles used for recreational purposes (snow-mobiles,
cross-country motor-cycles, motor-boats, private plans, etc.), but
also to the crowds of tourists themselves and the entertainments
provided for them (publicity stands, beach contests, etc.).

b) Loss of natural landscape; agricultural and pastoral lands

i) The growth of tourism brings with it the construction
of housing, facilities and infrastructure for tourists which inevitably
encroach on previously open spaces, i.e. on natural landscape or
agricultural or pastoral lands.

ii) Some valuable natural sites (beaches, forests) are often
barred to public access because they become privately owned by hotels
or individuals.

c) Destruction of flora and fauna

i) The various kinds of pollution mentioned above, together
with loss of natural landscape and agricultural and pastoral lands, are
responsible for the disappearance of some of the flora and fauna.

ii) Excessive access to and use of natural sites also result
in the disappearance of various plant and animal species, owing to
tourist behaviour (trampling, excessive picking of fruit or flowers,
carelessness, vandalism, or the kind of thoughtless conduct sometimes
leading to forest fires, for example).

24

d) Degradation of landscape and of historic sites and monuments

   i)   The installation of modern tourist-related facilities and
infrastructure often leads to aesthetic degradation of the landscape or
sites: the style and architecture of such new installations may thus
not always be in harmony or on a scale with traditional buildings,
moreover tourist facility development is often disorderly and scattered, giving the landscape a "moth-eaten" look.

   ii)   An excessive number of visitors to historical or exceptional natural sites may also result in degradation (graffiti, pilfering,
etc.).

e) Effects of congestion

   i)   The concentration in time and space of tourists on holiday
leads to congestion of beaches, ski slopes, resorts, and overloading
of tourist amenities and infrastructure, thus causing considerable harm
to the environment and detracting from the quality of life.

   ii)   One major consequence is traffic congestion on roads at
week-ends and at the beginning and end of peak holiday periods, leading
to loss of leisure time, high fuel consumption, and heavier air and
noise pollution.

f) Effects of conflict

   During the tourist season, the resident population not only has to
put up with the effects of such congestion, unknown during the rest of
the year, but often has to change its way of life completely (faster
work, pace, an extra occupation, etc.) and to live cheek by jowl with
people of a different, largely urban kind in search of leisure pursuits.
This "co-existence" is by no means always easy and social tensions,
particularly acute in places where there are many tourists, may occur.

g) Effects of competition

   Since the development of tourism uses up a great deal of space
and siphons off a fairly large proportion of local labour, competition is
bound to occur, usually to the detriment of traditional activities, for
(for instance, less land under cultivation and less manpower means
agriculture).

   Competition of this kind generally tends to result in the exclusive
practice of tourist-related activities, which may be economically
undesirable for the regions concerned.

While this classification of the impacts of tourism on the environment may be arbitrary, it has its uses since, on the one hand, it constitutes a kind of warning against mistakes made in the past due to excessive or poorly managed tourist development and, on the other hand, it suggests the type of actions to be taken in the future to meet the problems which arise in this domain.

Only a policy permitting the orientation and control of the growth of tourism can ensure the harmonious development of tourism with the environment. However the formulation of such a policy requires some knowledge or idea of how tourist and environmental needs will evolve.

Moreover, knowledge of this kind is also essential from the standpoint of environmental conservation; many case studies provide abundant evidence that environmental deterioration can usually be traced to lack of control of the fast-expanding tourism process.

In other words, it is vital that the growth of tourism should be controlled, which means that it must first be evaluated: how rapid will it be; where, when and in what form will it occur?

FUTURE PROSPECTS

The growth of tourism depends on a number of economic, sociological and political factors which, according to the way they evolve, may encourage or, retard the process.

A. Factors influencing tourism growth and their evolution

1. Economic factors

a) The rapid growth of disposable income in the OECD countries as a whole has provided greater access to leisure pursuits, and higher spending by tourists.

Although it has slowed since 1974 with the emergence of new economic problems, growth is still going on, and so continues to promote that of tourism, although to a lesser extent.

b) The growth of real GDP, which indicates variations in economic activity and real income levels, can be compared with the number of arrivals at frontiers and with international tourist receipts in real terms; these two indicators make it possible to evaluate variations in international tourism. This comparison brings out the following facts:

- economic conditions influence the evolution of international tourism;

26

- fluctuations in the tourism growth rate are more marked than in the GDP growth rate - a sign of a certain elasticity international tourism demand;
- overall and during a fairly long period (8-10 years), the rate of growth of international tourism however turns out to be higher than that of GDP or GNP: OECD figures thus show, along with a 4-5% growth rate for GNP in the OECD countries, around a 7% growth rate for tourism;
- whereas, between 1950 and 1975, the number of tourist arrivals for the world as a whole went up from 25 to 213 million (an annual growth rate of 8.9%), over the same period, the GWP (or Gross World Product of goods and services) rose by only 4.5% per year in constant dollars.

A United States estimate foresees, for the next 20 years, a 7% annual growth rate in international tourism expenditure, as against a relatively optimistic annual growth rate of 4.7% in GWP. *

If the annual growth rate of real GDP is some 4.5%, it may therefore be assured that the tourism growth rate will amount to at least some 6%.

Given the elasticity of the international tourism sector, its growth would only affected by unforeseen economic or political developments.

Demand for national tourism, on the other hand, appears to be much more rigid: a study of the trend in numbers of nights spent by non-foreign tourists in each OECD Member country shows that the growth rate, while often lower, is steadier, and that it was little affected by the 1974 economic crisis. **

This difference between international and national tourism may be explained by a change in behaviour which modified tourist flows. In periods of economic recession, tourists tend to prefer to spend their holidays on their national territory; since this is less costly, it means that people can continue to go on holiday even if their "tourism budget" is reduced.

Moreover, the close relation between disposable income per inhabitant and tourism demand accounts for the slow, regular progression of national tourism and suggests that present trends will continue in the coming years.

c) The normal reduction in working hours, due mainly to techno-logical developments in industry, means that more time is available

---

* Congress of the 11th ITB, Berlin, March 9-10, 1977, on the occasion of the 11th International Tourism-Exchange ITB Berlin, March 5-13, 1977. AMK Berlin, 157 p.
** Tourism Policy and International Tourism in OECD Member countries, OECD.

for tourism and leisure. Between 1968 and 1977, there has thus been a general reduction of four or more hours a week in the manufacturing industries in some European OECD Member countries and in Japan. * In Sweden and Finland, annual paid holidays have been increased from four to five weeks, and other OECD countries may well follow this example. The fact that retirement age is being progressively lowered likewise means that more spare time will be available.

d)   The lower relative cost of transport, especially car and air travel, and the consequent increase in motorization and mobility, contributed greatly to the expansion of tourism. According to the statistics of the International Civil Aviation Organisation, over the past ten years the number of passenger/kilometres has thus gone up by 9% per annum.

However, it may well happen owing to the big increase in fuel prices over the last five years, which is likely to continue, in future tourist trips will be fewer and shorter.

e)   The widespread improvement and extension of the infrastructure network, which facilitates access to tourist areas and, at the same time cuts travel time, is a major factor of tourist growth, particularly week-end tourism.

f)   Lastly, one long-term consequence of economic progress in the developing countries will be the arrival of new consumers on the tourism market.

*   REDUCTION IN PAID WORKING HOURS IN THE MANUFACTURING
INDUSTRIES OF SOME OECD COUNTRIES

COUNTRY	WEEKLY WORKING HOURS, 1968	WEEKLY WORKING HOURS, 1977	DIFFERENCE
Austria[1]	38.6	33.9	-4.7
France	45.3	41.3	-4.0
Japan	44.6	40.3	-4.3
Norway[2]	36.7	31.7	-5.0
Portugal[3]	44.7	40.1	-4.6
United Kingdom[2]	45.8	43.6	-2.2
Sweden[3]	38.7	33.2	-5.5

1.   Including the extractive industries.
2.   Men only.
3.   In 1976 instead of 1977.

SOURCE: Yearbook of Labour Statistics, International Labour Office, Geneva, 38th
        edition.

28

2. Sociological factors

a) <u>Increased urbanization and industrialization</u> in the OECD countries is largely responsible for deterioration of the living environment. A mark of the population response is the growing need for relaxation and a change of scene in unpolluted surroundings, for obvious reasons of health and mental well-being. As industrialization and, above all, urbanization are on the increase in most OECD countries, it is likely that holiday departure rates (related to urbanization rates)* will steadily increase.

b) This need or "demand for leisure" is increasingly sustained and even actively fostered <u>by the mass media and advertising</u> which are fast-expanding types of service sharpening a taste for travel and for the attractions of far-off, exotic lands and thus promote tourist growth as well as new kinds of travel.

c) The earlier-mentioned assumption, which was that higher fuel prices might modify or even reduce tourist travel, may be offset by the fact that when faced with a difficult economic situation, few consumers only are prepared to curtail expenditure on items such as travel, recreations and the use of the motor car.

In France, for example, higher petrom prices have not led to any lasting or significant reduction in road traffic. A survey by the weekly magazine "L'Express" in September 1978 shows that the holiday budget item is the last one on which French people would economize if they had to reduce their standard of living: 28% said they would save first on clothing and only 6% on holidays. In view of this attitude, it may be assumed that the number of tourists will continue to increase, in spite of unfavourable economic circumstances; at most, growth will slow only slightly.

---

* In 1977 the French newspaper "Vie Quotidienne" compiled statistics on holiday departure rates for French people according to place of residence:

Place of residence	Holiday departure rates
Rural communities	30.1%
Towns of less than 20,000 inhabitants	43.9%
Towns of 20,000 to 100,000 inhabitants	56.6%
Cities of 100,000 inhabitants and over, excluding Greater Paris	62.5%
Greater Paris	84.2%
City of Paris	85.8%

3. Policy factors

In view of the economic importance of the tourist sector in a number of OECD countries (see Part I. B b), the governments of these countries can be expected to continue policies to develop it; governments of other countries experiencing economic difficulties may also seek to adopt such policies with a view to:

- reducing unemployment through the creation of jobs,
- developing or reviving certain areas,
- above all, bridging the gap in their trade balance, due for the most part to fuel imports.

B. Some aspects of future tourist growth and consequences for the environment

1. Rate of growth

An assessment of the main factors influencing tourism demand and their probable trend hence suggests that overall growth will continue but at a slower rate (of some 6% per year, in view of the economic difficulties which may continue or emerge).

Furthermore, a real tourism boom occurred during the 1960's and it can be assumed that 20 to 30 age group of those years will retain their tourist expenditure habits; at the same time a new generation is coming on the tourist market. The result will be a steady rise in the number of tourists until the "new wave of the 60s" gradually ages and loses momentum around 1990 or 2000. From then on the growth of tourism could level out to a certain extent, all the more as the population of the industrialized countries, the main "generators" of tourists, could well decline.

This assumption concerning the growth of tourism is confirmed by projections drawn up by economists and experts in the tourism sector, by various international organisations and by many OECD countries:

a) A forecast covering the next 25 years* thus predicts a lower growth rate for international tourism (5% per year); domestic tourism will continue to grow, but slightly more slowly than at present.

b) UNEP experts predict an increase of 20 to 33 million tourists between now and 1985 for the northwest Mediterranean area (France,

---

* H. Hoffmann, "Berner Studien zum Fremdenverkehr", Vol. 12, Bern and Frankfurt, 1974, p. 22 and following pages.

Italy, Spain); this represents a yearly growth rate of 3.7% to 5%. *

c)   According to an ECE study, ** the number of tourists per metre of Mediterranean coastline in EEC countries will rise from 2.74 in 1974 to 5.04 by 1980, an annual increase of 4%.

d)   In respect of air traffic (a good indicator of tourist activity), the International Air Transport Association forecasts, for the period 1976-1982, a moderate growth rate of 6.3% annually for the North Atlantic and 6.5% for European traffic.   The Western European Airports Association foresees an average annual growth rate of 7.8% for the period 1976-1990 as against 10.1% for the period 1965-1975. Long-distance flights will have a higher yearly growth rate than short-distance flights (10.3% compared with 6.6%).

e)   Several OECD countries have provided information on their tourism growth rate, but only over the very short term:***

- Australia foresees an annual increase in foreign tourist arrivals of:
  10% in 1979
  8% in 1980.
- Finland foresees, for all types of accommodation, a total of 6.45 million nights in 1980 and 7.38 million in 1985 (an annual growth rate of 2.7%).
- In France, a survey by the Institut de Recherche en Informatique et en Economie (IRIEC) on the trend of seaside tourist demand for the period 1980-1990 puts forward four assumptions:
  - a "low" assumption of -0.3% annual growth for stays and -0.2% for days;
  - a "trend-based assumption with a growth of 3.5% for stays and 3.9% for days;
  - an assumption of permanent seaside urbanization, with a growth of 3.7% for stays and 4.2% for days;

   *   United Nations Environment Program, Tourism and the Environment in the Mediterranean Region: towards a better utilization of the tourism resources in the Mediterranean, Document UNEP/IG.5/INF 7 (UNEP, Geneva, 1976).
and : R. Baretjé, J.M. Thurot, Revue 2000, No.37, 1976.
   **   Methodology for Integrated Socio-Economic Environmental Planning of Tourist Industry Development: G. Fresco and others, ECE Symposium, Dubrovnik, 1978.
   ***   Tourism Policy and International Tourism in OECD Member countries, OECD, Paris, 1978.

- a "high" assumption, with an annual growth of 5. 1% for
  stays and 5. 9% for days. *

Moreover, for the 1985 horizon a holiday departure rate of
60% of the French population is foreseen; the present figure
is 54%.

- In Ireland, the annual growth rate for tourist numbers will
  be 3. 2% for the period 1978-1982, whereas that for tourist
  receipts will be 8. 2%.
- In New Zealand, the annual growth rate between 1978 and
  1982 will be 6% for both tourist arrivals and tourist receipts.
- Portugal expects tourism to go on growing at an annual rate
  of some 12% for nights spent by Portuguese tourists and
  over 7% for those spent by foreigners.
- For the United Kingdom, the National Tourist Board forecasts the following annual growth rates:

National tourism

	1977–1980	1980–1985	Annual growth rate
Stays	12%	15%	3. 2%
Nights	11%	18%	3. 4%
Tourist expen- diture (1977 prices).	13%	20%	4. 0%

International tourism

	1977–1980	1980–1985	1985–1990	Annual growth rate
Number	11%	33%	23%	4. 8%
Nights	6%	15%	23%	3. 2%

- In Switzerland, a fairly conservative long-term forecast
  puts the national and international tourism expansion rate
  at almost 4%. The number of nights spent, which was 66

---

    *   Les Perspectives du Tourisme sur le Littoral : Demande française et étrangère,
IRIEC, 1972, DATAR.

million in 1973, would thus increase to 100 million in 1983 and 200 million in 1990. *
- Turkey expects, for the period 1977-1982, an annual growth rate of 14. 5% for foreign visitors and 12. 9% for income.

Hence all these projections assume that tourism will continue to expand at a rate varying from one country to another but never far removed from the general 6% figure. Since in 1977 240 million tourist arrivals were recorded for the world as a whole, in 1990 this number would reach some 500 million. Even with a pessimistic assumption of slower growth rate of 3. 5%, there would still be nearly 400 million arrivals in 1990, meaning increased pressure on the environment.

This pressure will, however, vary in intensity according to the characteristics of future tourist growth, that is, geographic location, location in time, and the forms it takes.

2. The geographical factor

If tourist growth is more evenly spread over space - in other words, if the "new tourists" do not each year swell the already existing ranks, thus overloading those areas where tourism is already highly developed, then the pressure on the environment will be less intense, and tourism will be better assimilated by the host region.

While forecasting future tourist destinations is a risky undertaking, some assumptions can be attempted:

a)   Within the OECD area, traditional tourist flows towards Europe will probably undergo some change; there may well be a swing towards countries such as the United States, Canada, Australia and New Zealand, which are trying to compensate for distance by offering very attractive air fares and promoting tours.

b)   There may be an upswing in the number of stays in exotic and developing countries owing to:

- lower long-distance air travel rates;
- favourable exchange rates and moderate living costs in the developing countries;
- desire for a change of scene and growing interest in these countries;
- overcrowding at traditional resorts, particularly in Western Europe, visited by 2/3 of the world's tourists.

---

*   Objectives and Measures for achieving planned tourism development, P. Keller, ECE.

There is thus an increasing demand for as yet untouched environments, particularly islands: tour operators, are hence trying to develop and organise cruise facilities, a very profitable tourism product, since the cost of hotel accommodation is rising all the time.

This "shift" of tourism towards new countries will therefore bring some minor relief to traditional tourist areas; but to hitherto unspoiled places, the pollution and degradation produced by tourism will be transferred.

c) This process, already noted on an international scale, is also happening at national level owing to the growing demand for "nature tourism". This type of tourism, which calls for natural sites still untouched, may add still further to the areas already subjected to intensive tourism and therefore to environmental degradation.

This kind of tourism (hiking, cross-country skiing, bicycle tours, horse back riding) presumably will have but a limited impact on the environment, since little is required in the way of facilities. Moreover those who enjoy these pursuits seek an environment of outslanding quality and may therefore reasonably be expected to look after it.

d) At national level, it seems likely that the excessive development of traditional tourist resorts, with all the consequences it entails (overcrowding, inordinate financial charges, intensive environmental deterioration, etc.) will induce national authorities to set up new tourist areas, as has been done in France along the Languedoc-Roussillon and Aquitaine coasts.

e) This would also enable regional development to be brought into better economic balance, insofar as tourism might compensate for or even arrest, the decline of areas which are disadvantaged in the matter of resources or activities.

f) Lastly, along with the demand for seaside holidays which still predominates, * new kinds of tourism may perhaps develop calling for a type of environment other than that of traditional tourist areas, whose burden will thus be lightened. A case in point is "waterway tourism" along French and English rivers and canals, and another is "rural tourism", now becoming increasingly popular in the countryside, well away from any beaten track, particularly in Germany, Austria and France.

While a better geographical "spread" of tourism is thus conceivable it is impossible to say whether this will be sufficient to absorb the annual tourist surplus and prevent excessive pressure on certain local environments.

---

*   According to a survey carried out by the French weekly "L'Express", in September 1978, 49% of French people holidaying in France went to the seaside, and 20% to mountain areas.

34

3. The time factor

Another good way of avoiding environmental deterioration is to
stagger the tourist season.

Several countries are striving to stagger holidays, but so far there
have been no significant results, and it is unlikely that the situation
will change very much in the short term, in view of the obstacles to such
a policy: weather, school terms and holidays, firms' operating sched-
ules, habit, etc.

It may, however, be assumed that in the long term holidays will
be more evenly spread out over the year, because:

- tourism development in far-away places will call for off-season
  holidays (particularly in winter for the northern hemisphere);
- this also applies to the development of winter sports, and the
  number of skiers throughout the world is yearly expected to
  rise by 6. 8% during the period 1976-1982.
  In France, the annual growth rate for winter-sport departures
  was 7. 1% between 1958 and 1968, and 8. 4% between 1968 and
  1978;
- while it is true that in several countries the rate of holiday
  departures of rural populations has risen considerably, the
  consequences for the environment of this increase in the number
  of tourists will be negligible, since farmers are obliged to take
  their holidays at off-peak times - in winter, for instance;
- staggering tourist departures means that installations and
  infrastructure can be used to the full, thus bringing increased
  profitability; in addition, it reduces the losses due to the
  effects of congestion (leisure time, energy resources, over-
  equipment, etc.). For these purely economic reasons, national
  authorities as well as tour producers and operators are increasingly trying to encourage the staggering of holidays in many
  ways:

  - in a number of countries, off-season air fares are less
    expensive;
  - in France, a directive recommends that holiday accommoda-
    tion should be rented weekly rather than monthly, thus provid-
    ing for greater flexibility;
  - the Netherlands and Germany have concluded bilateral agree-
    ments on the staggering of school holidays;
  - in most countries, special offers of off-season rates by
    hoteliers and carriers.

Such incentives further stimulate a trend towards the staggering
of holidays which has recently been developing spontaneously among
some tourists, because the disamenities of seasonal concentration

(effects of overcrowding, overpopulation, shortages, etc.) are becoming ever harder to endure.

For all these reasons, holidays are being broken down into much shorter stays which are more evenly spread over the year but also more frequent.

It seems likely that this new tendency will, of itself, become more marked, and that it will also be encouraged by governments as all the resulting advantages begin to make themselves felt.

Less seasonal concentration will be excellent for the environment, since numerous case studies show that too many tourists in the same place at the same time has been one of the fundamental causes of environmental deterioration.

But a greater number of shorter stays also promotes a kind of tourism whose impact on the environment appears to be particularly harmful, since certain types of area as well as infrastructure and transport facilities are then more heavily used.

This is week-end tourism, increasingly popular in most OECD countries, as can be seen from the more and more frequent traffic congestions outside large cities on Friday and Sunday evenings. France, Germany and the United Kingdom expect over-occupancy of middle-range flights because of this uptrend in week-end tourism in the years to come. An EEC study[*] foresees that in 1980 a city-dweller will need from 100 to 300 m^2 of peri-urban open space, and a tourist 750 m^2 of space for recreational purposes. Overall needs for all the ECE countries for space for leisure, holidays and week-ends will reach some 13,500 to 19,000 km^2 by 1980, accounting for 2% of these countries' agricultural and pastoral land; housing, hotels and similar establishments for tourists will cover another 650 to 1,000 km2, so that the total land area taken up by tourism will be of the order of 45,000 to 85,000 km2.

Since week-end tourism has developed largely because of the need to compensate for urban living conditions, it is probable that it will keep pace with the growth of urbanization. There is another contributory factor: because of economic difficulties, certain categories of tourists are obliged to cut down on the length of their holiday and the distance away from home; these categories will be more inclined to go away for the week-end.

If week-end tourism goes on growing at this rate, three types of environmental deterioration threaten during the coming years:

---

[*]   "Besoins de détente en tant que facteurs pour le développement régional et agricole", EEC, Directorate-General for Agriculture, No.116, November 1973. (No English text exists).

- the almost total destruction of scarce urban and peri-urban open spaces due to overuse; many forests and woods which make up the "green belt" around large urban centres thus show signs of degeneration, and the fact that they are now managed solely for recreational purposes has completely altered the natural reproduction cycle of the trees;
- increased pollution, due to the widespread use of private cars to reach these areas;
- heavier consumption of the peri-urban areas still available, both because of the increasing amount of space taken up by infrastructure (particularly the motorway network), whose capacity will be increased so as to reduce travelling time, and because of the growing number of secondary residences, the most convenient type of accommodation for week-end tourism, but also the most space-consuming.

4. Future forms of tourism

As the impact on the environment also varies according to the type of tourism involved, it is important to try to see how space will be used by tourism in forthcoming years.

This type of forecasting is particularly difficult, since future forms of tourism depend essentially on how tourist patterns evolve, while these also are hard to predict, since they too are subject to change and are influenced by factors of all kinds (fashions, economic conditions, etc.).

Taking present changes as a starting-point, it is however possible to detect the main trends. Long-term government action to channel the growth of tourism along certain lines also provides a clue to the forms future tourism will take.

i) In regard to types of accommodation and services, the most striking feature of demand seems to be that quality and comfort - not to say luxury - are ever-growing requirements. One mark of this is the proliferation and high occupancy rate of hotels of a certain standard; another is the development at resorts, of seasonal shops dealing in luxury goods.

Such a demand for quality and taste for amenities, acquired as the standard of living rises, will most likely increase or at least be maintained as time goes on.

Such a trend could benefit to the environment, since supply will have to be adapted to demand and a higher-quality product provided, which means that accommodation conditions, sanitation facilities, architecture, etc., will improve.

Moreover, tour producers and operators will have to meet the wishes and requirements of countries and resort areas, which are increasingly aware of the environmental damage threatened by tourism development.

Environmental protection is therefore becoming one of their main concerns, and their aim how is better integration of tourism into the local environment coupled with a higher profitability, the present tendency being to group tourist accommodation and facilities so as to preserve open space, reduce disamenities and pollution, and improve architectural quality.

Such an improvement in the standard of tourist accommodation and amenities is strongly encouraged by many governments, who have made it one of the leading aims of their tourist policy:

- Austria, for instance, is seeking to improve accommodation and service conditions by avoiding overconcentration in certain areas, providing more indoor entertainment for tourists, and improving vocational training;
- Ireland is aiming at improvements in vocational training, services, reception and the dissemination of information;
- Italy, Luxembourg, Switzerland, Turkey and Yugoslavia are encouraging modernization and improved quality of service and facilities, largely through subsidies;

In coming years action by tourists, tour producers and authorities could hence combine to bring about a substantial improvement in tourist accommodation and amenities, with beneficial effects for the environment and for living conditions during the tourist season.

ii) Paradoxically, these quality requirements go hand in hand with price requirements. While high-quality accommodation and services are demanded, the tourist would seem to insist that they be inexpensive. There are three reasons for this change of attitude:

- the tourist is armed with fuller information about the "holidays and leisure" product he wants to consume, and is more exacting in his choice;
- low-income groups account for an increasing proportion of overall tourist demand, and can consume only an inexpensive product;
- moreover, groups which, owing to economic difficulties are cutting down on their tourist expenditure, increasingly seek a less expensive product, yet expect it to be of the same quality they were accustomed to before.

Reasonably-priced types of tourist accommodation have therefore rapidly developed, such as small hotels, simple accommodation in rural areas, furnished rented accommodation, board and lodging with local people and, above all, camping and caravaning, marked by a spectacular uptrend in many countries.

In France, for instance, the number of places available in camp-sites went up by 56% between 1970 and 1977, and another 800,000 places are planned over the next few years. *

Germany foresees that by 1990 the number of caravans will have increased tenfold, bringing the total up to 2 1/2 million.

For obvious reasons of social policy, many countries are looking for ways to encourage development of these inexpensive types of accommodation. But unless this policy is backed up by strict regula-tions, particularly in the matter of sanitary installations, severage, restriction of accommodation capacity, etc. , may well occur and bring serious environmental deterioration in their wake. This is because the low return from this kind of accommodation often means that little or no upkeep and modernization can be undertaken, unless subsidies or low-interest loans are available, as they are in some countries (Austria, France, Iceland, Italy, Japan, Switzerland).

iii) Alongside development of this type of "social" accom-modation, there is spontaneous proliferation of secondary residences in a number of OECD countries. The countries most affected by the trend are those with extensive and varied tourist assets, such as France; and those where per capita income is high and individual housing is widely preferred, such as the Scandinavian countries.

It is thus estimated that the yearly rate of increase for secondary residences in some OECD countries will be as follows:

France .... 7. 2% between 1970 and 1980
Sweden .... 2. 8% between 1969 and 1990
Norway .... 4. 7% between 1969 and 1990
Denmark .... 8. 0% between 1969 and 1985

Even if this trend is not generally widespread, its potential impact on the environment should be taken into account, owing to concomitant effects, especially of a negative kind:

- eating up of the landscape,
- heavy consumption of space for merely seasonal use,
- disruption of the urban pattern,
- increased cost of infrastructure,
- increase of private ownership, which often means that access to outstanding scenic sites is barred to the public (shores, beaches, etc.), thus contributing to overconcentration.

---

* Statement by V. Giscard d'Estaing in the "Charte de la Qualité de la Vie" (Charter for the Quality of Life).

Only effective regulations, such as those in force in Austria, can arrest this trend and the resulting environmental deterioration. Austria has successfully put into effect a policy of loans with very low interest rates, for small hotels and furnished accommodation while, at the same time discouraging the construction of secondary residences by imposing stringent requirements.

iv)   In respect to types of tourism, the demand is growing for nature tourism and open-air recreational activities, particularly in countries with a high rate of urbanization, such as the Scandinavian countries, the United States, Canada, the Netherlands, the United Kingdom, and Japan, where it is estimated that the demand for open-air leisure pursuits will double or triple in the next 10 years. The very nature of this type of tourism, which calls for few if any facilities but requires a high-quality environment, helps to protect the resort area.

For this reason, tourist policies in many countries aim to encourage this new movement through such various measures as the creation of nature reserves and national parks, particularly in Australia, France, Japan, the United Kingdom.

One consequence of this new tourist demand is the recent development of rural tourism, increasingly popular because it satisfies the need for contact with the natural environment and is inexpensive. Since, it has the added advantage of not damaging the environment while contributing to regional development, certain countries are attaching more and more importance to this type of tourism:*

-    in rural tourism housing which already exists is used for accommodation, thus reducing investment costs and avoiding the consumption of space still available and any major changes to the environment;
-    moreover, as such inexpensive holidays, usually spent in areas rarely visited by tourists, help to diversify the supply, and tourist activities are spread more evenly over the national territory; this has happened in Austria and Yugoslavia. Not only is this good for the environment; it also provides the local economy with appreciable extra income;
-    lastly, since tourist amenities are developed and organised by local people - householders or small family businesses - the revenue from tourism directly benefits the local population, instead of being diverted, as so often happens when large tourist resorts are run by operators from outside. Earnings are then ploughed back on the spot, making it possible to improve accommodation and modernize installations.

*   "Development of tourism at regional level and in rural areas" - Tourism Policy and International Tourism in OECD Member countries, OECD, Paris, 1978, pp. 31-32.

Hence the development of rural tourism does not threaten the environment, largely because, unlike in mass tourism, widely scattered small units are involved.

On the whole, then, the broad lines along which new forms of tourism are developing seem fairly favourable for purposes of environmental conservation. But, like the spontaneous trends governing tourism development in terms of volume, space and time, these new forms will have to be carefully watched; if they are to evolve in a manner and at a pace consistent with environmental needs, permanent government supervision may even be necessary.

Tourism is thus involving more and more people and becoming a virtual mass phenomenon whose uncontrolled expansion can be seriously damaging for the environment. Effective organisation and regulations are thus essential; hence it is vital for governments to know what the future prospects for tourism are so that they can adopt long-term policies in order to intensify, modify or check trends in tourism growth in line with environmental requirements.

THE SPANISH EXAMPLE

A. Growth of tourism in Spain

In the case of Spain, studies carried out by the authorities indicate that future trends will be similar to those forecast for the Mediterranean as a whole; the number of foreign tourists will continue to grow, slowly but steadily.

Spanish government policy on the future of tourism is to maximize revenue from tourism, with minimum damage to the environment. This it is planned to achieve without adding significantly to the number of foreign tourists, and also that tourism will have to be spread more evenly over the whole year.

The Spanish analysis, however, forecasts a significant increase in domestic tourism. Over the last few years, there has already been some increase, at a more rapid pace than for international tourism. In 1978 it was thus estimated that the number of domestic tourists was some 18 million, and to this figure must be added that for international tourists, estimated at 38 million. It is therefore hardly surprising that the problems raised by such a considerable tourists flow should take on major proportions, especially as tourism is concentrated in certain limited areas.

41

B. Measurement of the regional distribution of tourism

It has been possible to determine leading tourist regions and their order of importance by using several indices: tourist capacity and density, hotel density and intensity, and the market share of each area in percentage terms.

TOURIST CAPACITY
(According to region)

Index

Costa Brava 27. 7
Majorca 13. 6
Costa del Sol 10. 5
Grand Canary Island 8. 0
Barcelona 6. 7
Madrid 4. 5
Murcia - Alicante 3. 6
Tenerife 2. 3
San Sebastian 2. 0
Santander 1. 0

$$\text{Tourist capacity} = \frac{\begin{array}{c}\text{No. of beds} \\ \text{main hotels} \\ \text{etc.}\end{array} + \begin{array}{c}\text{No. of places of} \\ \text{restaurants} \\ \text{etc.}\end{array} + \begin{array}{c}\text{No. of} \\ \text{commercial} \\ \text{licences}\end{array}}{\begin{array}{c}\text{Normal population} \\ \text{in '000s}\end{array} \times \begin{array}{c}\text{Land area} \\ \text{km}^2\end{array}} \times 100$$

TOURIST DENSITY
(According to region)

Index

Majorca 827
Costa Brava 248
Tenerife 143
Great Canary Islands 122
Costa del Sol 113
Murcia Alicante 45
Barcelona 14
Madrid 13
San Sebastian   9
Santander   5

42

$$\text{Tourist Density (TD)} = \frac{5\, u_i\, w_i}{D} \times \frac{P_e}{P_t}$$

TD	=	index of tourist density
u_i	=	number of places in category i hotels
w_i	=	weight of the number of places in category i in total
D	=	normal population of the region
P_e	=	number of nights spent by foreigners
P_t	=	total number of nights in the region

HOTEL DENSITY		HOTEL INTENSITY	
1. Costa Brava	62. 32	1. Majorca	407. 09
2. Majorca	56. 68	2. Costa Brava	178. 90
3. Great Canary Islands	27. 58	3. Great Canary Islands	57. 59
4. Tenerife	9. 96	4. Costal del Sol	54. 37
5. Barcelona	8. 22	5. Tenerife	54. 13
6. Costa del Sol	6. 48	6. Murcia - Alicante	32. 93
7. Madrid	5. 96	7. Santander	18. 50
8. San Sebastian	3. 79	8. Barcelona	16. 17
9. Murcia - Alicante	3. 36	9. Madrid	12. 56
10. Santander	1. 63	10. San Sebastian	11. 98

Hotel density: Also indicates the hotel potential of a region expressed in terms of places available per km2 of surface area, overall or by category.

Hotel intensity: Indicates the hotel potential of a region, expressed in terms of places available per 1,000 permanent residents, overall or by category.

MARKET SHARE OF THE VARIOUS REGIONS, IN %

1.	Majorca	35. 20
2.	Murcia - Alicante	7. 40
3.	Madrid	7. 47
4.	Barcelona	6. 83
5.	Costa del Sol	6. 36
6.	Costa Brava	5. 55
7.	Tenerife	5. 11
8.	Great Canary Islands	4. 67
9.	Santander	0. 76
10.	San Sebastian	0. 75

If these various indices are combined, the ten tourist regions can be classified in the following order: Majorca, Costa Brava, Great Canary Islands, Costa del Sol, Tenerife, Barcelona, Murcia-Alicante, Madrid, Santander and San Sebastian. This classification shows that relatively small geographical regions may have a relatively high average density, with all the consequences that this entails.

Serious difficulties were also generated in these areas, due to two other factors: the extraordinarily high demand for services was crowded into a few months, and the relatively small local population lacked the resources to supply adequate services.

Furthermore, the Spanish government is well aware that tourist regions in Spain suffer from certain shortcomings, some of which are listed below:

- overexploitation of tourist resources;
- damage to nature and to the environment;
- inadequate infrastructure;
- shortcomings in supporting local and commercial services;
- poor land use, including that of coastal areas;
- inadequate building laws and overconcentration of people in tourist areas.

Without seeking to excuse these shortcomings, it is only fair to say that tourism in Spain was developed in economically and socially underdeveloped regions, ill prepared for orderly adaptation to the process; until recently, the application of land-use and environmental measures was not widespread. It must also be recognized that, when tourism development began, Spain was experiencing balance-of-payment difficulties and was accordingly inclined to give priority to improving the balance. Furthermore, the lack of public funds at both central and local government level meant that the investments needed for providing adequate infrastructure could not be made.

C.   The measures proposed

For all these reasons, the Spanish government intends to launch a whole series of measures (several are already underway) concerning land-use policies in tourist areas. These measures are intended either for remedying damage already done or for planning future land use. The remedial measures have consequently been taken in previously developed tourist areas, while the planning measures will affect the undeveloped regions.

Surveys of tourist areas are to be carried out, in order to obtain the following data:

- examination of the present supply of tourist services;
- examination of existing infrastructure and present urban development;
- examination of existing difficulties in government and market services;
- inventory and evaluation of tourist resources;
- study of potential tourist demand and origin of tourists;
- establishment of areas suited to the development of tourist facilities;
- study and classification of areas in terms of environmental protection requirements;
- environmental protection measures;
- establishment of tourist itineraries;
- harmonization of tourism planning with nature and environmental conservation requirements;
- alternative land uses compatible with tourism;
- evaluation of possible benefits to local populations.

In 1977 the Secretariat of State for Tourism began to draft an outline law on tourism and to implement, region by region, a country-wide programme for the supply of tourist services.

Three aspects are covered:

a)   Inventory of tourism resources in areas where there is as yet little pressure from tourism and where no significant growth is foreseen.

b)   Planning the supply of tourist services in areas where these facilities have already been considerably developed and where urban congestion problems may arise; also where the increased profitability of seasonal activities may lead to problems of protecting the environment and natural resources.

c)   Plans for tourism development in developing or undeveloped areas with a substantial tourism potential.

In these areas orderly planning may strongly influence both tourism development and town planning, since new plans can still be freely implemented to some extent.

The programme's short-term aim is to obtain as much information as possible on the various measures which should be taken now by the administrative authorities concerned; in the medium term, the objective is to draw up a complete inventory of the various policy instruments and study how they can best be used (this will take six years).

The long-term aim is to adapt land-use planning to the requirements of tourism development policy. Under Spanish law, the following minimum requirements for infrastructure are laid down:

- drinking water supply,
- sewage treatment and waste water disposal,
- electric power,
- communications,
- car parks,
- treatment and disposal of solid waste.

Power and communications problems have been solved in all regions, including those where tourism development has already taken place. For the other four items, there are still obvious gaps, which the Spanish Government is prepared to deal with.

Since 1972, plans on a national scale have been in preparation for the installation of a sewerage system covering the tourist areas along the Mediterranean coast. These plans, which will cost 21 billion pesetas, have recently been put in hand, and part of the work is now completed. Conflicts between the central government, the autonomous Spanish provinces and local authorities as to their respective jurisdiction, together with the huge sums required for these investments, have meant that final responsibility falls on the central government.

In future, however, it is considered that local authorities will be in a stronger financial position to meet tourist needs, largely because of various measures to reform local taxation systems, which will bring in additional revenue.

In the matter of environmental protection it should be pointed out that only recently has Spain joined the ranks of the economically developed countries. A country devoid of major industrial centres and overdeveloped urban areas has no environmental problems.

When industrialization and urban concentration did take place in Spain, environmental problems arose to which solutions are still being sought. But, that tourism should inevitably bring about actual deterioration of the environment, cannot be accepted. In theory, tourism should not be a cause of environmental deterioration, and it should be remembered that in general tourism gravitates towards areas barely touched by industry and which have largely retained their natural features. It is therefore essential that the programmes, particularly those concerning the environment, be based on the tourist flows into a given region rather than on the size of the area's normal population.

A general distinction between tourism and nature conservation should be made:

- there are those who argue that access to areas of outstanding natural value should be either prohibited or so limited as to result in zero damage to the environment;
- in the meantime, one tourism objective should be to keep the use of natural areas down to such a level as to preserve an irreplaceable national heritage for future generations;

- while the public should be given the widest possible access to natural areas, the environment must be protected to the utmost.

Following the administrative reform of 1977, the Spanish Government emphasized its concern with environmental issues, and an Under-Secretariat for Land-Use Policy was set up. At the same time, a new lease of life was given to the Interministerial Commission for the Environment (CIMA), which includes a Special Committee for Tourism and Environment.

Tourist resources to be protected can be divided into four types of environment:

1. Aquatic (watercourses and their banks, oceans, seas, coasts and coastal waters, aquatic animal and plant life).
2. Terrestrial (land and soil, wildlife, countryside, air).
3. Architectural (man-made structures attracting tourists because of their special features and purposes.
4. Human (human activities which can be appreciated in terms unrelated to their specific purpose or physical environment).

The first two categories clearly coincide with traditional environmental concerns. Authorities responsible for tourism have become increasingly anxious to safeguard and restore the environment as tourism has grown.

For this reason the programme drawn up by the Ministry of Commerce and Industry consists of three parts:

1. Preparation of an inventory of basic tourist resources.
2. Implementation of measures to conserve resources listed in the inventory.
3. Measures to ensure that such resources are best used in connection with tourism development.

II

THE ECONOMIC ASPECTS OF ENVIRONMENTAL PROTECTION IN TOURISM *

INTRODUCTION

This paper presents and discusses the major economic issues relevant to environmental protection in tourism. The view taken here is that tourism constitutes an important sector in the majority of OECD countries and makes significant contributions to these countries economies. Table 1 provides some indication of the relative importance of tourism for the balance of payments. Environmental resources are major inputs into this sector and economic policy measures could be used to ensure that these resources are used efficiently according to the long term requirements of the tourist sector, the tourist regions and the nation as a whole.

It is fully recognized that there are other and equally important aspects of tourism, e. g. social, cultural, etc. Furthermore, it is also acknowledged that economic measures are only one set of policy instruments which governments might use in the field of tourism. In addition the paper deals only with a limited aspects of the economic features of tourism, namely with those directly relevant to environment.

The paper consists of three main parts:

a)   Part I presents the main economic features of tourism considering it from the point of the environment. Tourism is given here a very broad definition, the emphasis being however on those tourists whose recreational, leisure, sporting and cultural activities have considerable impact on the environment. Similarly the environment and environmental protection are given the broadest interpretation: reduction of the various polluting activities to safeguard the health of the population and minimize material damage, protection of fauna and flora, conservation of green areas and coastal belts and the safeguarding of the natural heritage.

b)   Part II examines the hypothesis that environmental degradation in certain tourist areas reached such a proportion that tourism is now

---

*   Report by the Secretariat.

Table 1
SHARE OF INTERNATIONAL TOURIST RECEIPTS IN EXPORTS OF GOODS AND SERVICES

(In %)

RECEIVING COUNTRIES	1972	1973	1974	1975	1976	1977	AVERAGE 1972/77
EUROPE	6.4	5.9	4.8	5.3	5.1	(5.4)	5.5
Spain	32.6	30.9	24.7	25.0	21.3	23.1	26.3
Austria	27.2	26.0	20.4	23.3	23.5	21.7	23.7
Greece	20.7	19.1	12.6	16.2	18.5	(19.6)	17.8
Portugal	18.5	17.8	14.0	12.1	12.7	(14.0)	14.8
Switzerland	11.8	11.5	10.0	10.3	9.7	(9.3)	10.4
Italy	9.2	8.7	6.5	7.2	6.7	8.2	7.8
Ireland	8.3	7.6	7.3	6.7	5.9	(5.1)	6.8
Denmark	7.8	6.6	5.9	6.2	6.2	6.5	6.5
Turkey	5.3	5.6	5.4	5.5	7.0	(7.8)	6.1
Finland	6.4	6.3	4.6	4.8	4.3	4.0	5.1
France	5.5	5.1	4.3	5.0	4.9	(5.3)	5.0
United Kingdom	3.6	3.5	3.2	3.8	4.2	4.5	3.8
Norway	3.4	2.8	2.4	3.1	3.2	3.3	3.0
Germany	3.3	2.8	2.2	2.6	2.6	2.7	2.7
Netherlands	3.5	3.2	2.5	2.6	2.2	2.1	2.7
Iceland	2.7	3.1	3.3	2.5	2.1	(2.1)	2.6
Belgium-Luxembourg	2.2	2.3	1.9	2.2	2.0	2.0	2.1
Sweden	1.7	1.6	1.5	1.7	1.6	(2.0)	1.7
NORTH AMERICA	4.2	3.7	3.2	3.5	3.7	3.5	3.6
Canada	5.0	4.7	4.4	4.5	4.3	3.8	4.4
United States	3.9	3.4	2.9	3.3	3.6	3.4	3.4
AUSTRALASIA - JAPAN	0.9	0.9	0.8	0.8	0.8	(0.8)	0.8
New Zealand	3.1	3.4	4.5	5.7	4.8	(4.3)	4.3
Australia	1.9	1.8	2.1	2.0	2.0	2.3	2.0
Japan	0.6	0.5	0.4	0.4	0.4	0.4	0.4
OECD	5.3	4.8	3.9	4.3	4.2	(4.4)	4.5

SHARE OF INTERNATIONAL TOURIST EXPENDITURE IN IMPORTS OF GOODS AND SERVICES

(In %)

GENERATING COUNTRIES	1972	1973	1974	1975	1976	1977	AVERAGE 1972/77
EUROPE	5.4	5.3	4.1	4.8	4.7	(4.9)	4.9
Austria	8.6	7.7	7.7	9.0	10.3	10.0	8.9
Germany	8.8	9.3	7.8	8.6	7.9	8.3	8.4
Switzerland	6.1	6.2	5.6	6.6	6.6	(5.8)	6.1
Denmark	6.0	5.3	4.4	5.1	5.0	5.7	5.3
Sweden	6.7	5.7	4.0	4.4	4.6	(5.0)	5.1
Norway	5.1	4.5	4.0	4.7	4.9	5.3	4.8
Portugal	5.5	6.0	4.6	5.8	3.0	(2.5)	4.6
France	4.8	4.6	3.7	4.6	4.4	(4.8)	4.5
Ireland	4.9	4.6	4.0	4.8	4.2	(3.7)	4.4
Netherlands	4.4	4.3	3.5	4.1	4.1	4.7	4.2
Finland	4.1	4.1	2.8	3.3	3.7	3.9	3.7
Belgium - Luxembourg	3.9	4.0	3.1	3.6	3.3	3.4	3.6
Iceland	3.8	3.8	3.4	3.0	3.8	(3.4)	3.5
Turkey	3.0	3.5	3.2	3.1	3.6	(3.9)	3.4
United Kingdom	3.6	3.4	2.4	2.8	2.6	2.4	2.9
Greece	3.4	2.5	2.4	2.7	2.4	(2.8)	2.7
Spain	3.3	3.4	1.8	2.1	2.0	2.5	2.5
Italy	3.4	3.1	1.8	2.0	1.4	1.6	2.2
NORTH AMERICA	6.3	5.6	4.5	5.1	4.8	4.4	5.1
Canada	5.8	5.7	4.9	5.6	6.3	6.4	5.8
United States	6.4	5.6	4.4	4.9	4.3	3.9	4.9
AUSTRALASIA - JAPAN	3.5	3.3	2.4	2.5	2.6	(2.8)	2.9
New Zealand	6.3	6.6	5.5	5.2	5.5	(6.1)	5.9
Australia	5.1	4.6	3.6	4.3	3.9	3.3	4.1
Japan	2.9	2.8	1.9	2.0	2.2	2.6	2.4
OECD	5.5	5.2	4.0	4.6	4.4	(4.5)	4.7

( ) Estimates.

SOURCE: Tourism Policy and International Tourism in OECD Member countries, OECD, Paris, 1978.

declining in these areas. This examination is based largely on the information obtained from the case studies prepared by Member countries specifically for such an analysis. * Certain other information available from similar studies in this field has also been included.

c)   Part III examines the economic measures used in the case studies for their usefulness in protecting the environment, while ensuring at the same time the long term profitability of the tourist industry. These measures aim, through the use of the pricing mechanism and the application of the polluter-pays-principle, at protecting the environment from recurring, continuous pollution as well as from long run gradual degradation. In addition a number of other proposals are also put forward based on the experiences in environmental policy making in the industrial and transport sector. Finally, other measures, which, if adopted and implemented at the international level, could make useful contribution to environmental protection, are also put forward.

THE PRAGMATIC ECONOMICS OF TOURISM AND THEIR ENVIRONMENTAL IMPLICATIONS

It is convenient and useful to present the problem of environmental protection and the possible implications of environmental neglect in terms of economic behaviour of the main four actors in tourism: the consumer or the tourist; the direct producer and seller of tourist services, who is usually the private enterpreneur; the indirect producer of many of the services the tourist consumes, that is the local or regional government; and the national government carrying the overall responsibility to all these actors including the nation as a whole.

It is possible to provide an economic framework which prescribes how these actors should be behaving to ensure both the growth of tourism and environmental protection. Within the same framework it is also feasible to demonstrate, to describe that the pursuance of short-run interests by these groups could lead to environmental degradation and to a long-run decline in tourism.

The environmental objectives in tourists areas might be classified in the following categories:

i)   the protection of the health of the population, both touristic and local; the requirements under this heading refer to air and water quality requirements, the disposal of household waste and the maintenance of noise standards. The level of these standards should be at least as high as in the industrial

---

*   For the list of case studies see Appendix I.

areas where the tourists normally reside. Indeed a good
argument can be made out for higher standards on the grounds
that tourists are entitled to a better than normal environment
in order to recuperate. In addition a good tourist environment usually also implies a degree of tourist, or habitation
density which is consistent with a relaxed, healthy human
environment;

ii) in addition to the short term requirements described above
the environment should be maintained in a state, which should
ensure the long-term profitability of the industry. This is
more of a dynamic than static concept and even at any one
time tastes are vastly different; e. g. between the solitary
mountain climber and the gamblers of Las Vegas. Nevertheless it is fair to assume, that with increasing urbanization of
our industrial societies, there will be a long term demand for
a different and more human environment than the every day
urbanized habitat. This will require foresight and longer term
planning than was possible so far;

iii) consistent with the above objectives are certain national aims
which directly influence the tourist environment; these could
be manifold and for various purposes. Some areas could be
retained for the primary industry, providing at the same time
a 'green background' to the tourist area. In other cases it
would mean the preservation of a cultural heritage in form of
a venacular architecture or historic buildings. Or it may
signify the desire to protect a certain life style. In some
countries even legislation has been passed to preserve pristine
areas valued by that society for its unique natural characteristics.

The approach, normative and positive, employed here to prescribe
the optimal conditions and then describe the actual operation in tourism,
is useful because it leads logically to the type of economic measures
which would approximate the optimal situation.

The operation of the tourist sector

This section prescribes first the framework in which the environmental conditions laid down might be achieved and states the conditions
that needed to be fulfilled. Then it goes on to describe how the market
is most likely to operate and why is it unlikely that the environmental
objectives will be obtained when all the actors in tourism pursue their
separate short-term aims.

a) To obtain the environmental and economic objectives simultaneously the prescriptive framework is a market situation which tourist
authorities should try to establish; the main condition is that all actors

within this framework are maximizing certain interests <u>in the longer-term</u>. It is at the same time recognized that only few of these conditions are satisfied at any one time.

i) the consumer-tourist aims at obtaining maximum satisfaction for his expenditure; for this purpose he must acquire sufficient amount of information and expend time and effort to make the right choice. In addition to the information requirements he should have the knowledge of alternatives open to him to recoup his losses if the product (holiday) provided is different from the one he is contracted for. As a rational consumer he should be aware of the various health/environmental dangers he is facing in the area of his choice (air, water quality, congestion, etc.) and the possible benefits - financial and environmental - by changing the date and place of tourist activities;

ii) the private producer in the tourist sector should aim for long-term profit maximization both in the rate of development of the area, in the quality of the facilities constructed and in the type of development he is promoting. The maximization of long-term profits, rather than the maximization of tourist numbers in the short run would take into account the maintenance of the environment and the long term profitability of the area. The short-run profit maker is not motivated to take any of the above considerations into account and is likely to use up the environmental resources in an inefficient but from his point of view profitable way;

iii) the local and regional governments, the producer of indirect tourist services, should aim for the long-term maximization of income for the inhabitants of the region. This would include the provision and maintenance of employment from the tourist industry and income of the local inhabitants related to the tourist industry. Again it is in the long term interest of the local population that the economic viability of the industry is ensured. The second major economic objective of the local government is to ensure that the appropriate level of government expenditure for local, including environmental, services is financed to the maximum possible extent from charges imposed on the tourist sector and perhaps subsequently on the tourists. Such a policy would to a degree, ensure that a price is charged for environmental resources, that funds are available for environmental services and that the rate development is consistent with physical and fiscal resources available in the region;

iv) the national government carries an overall responsibility for the economic management and for balanced regional development. For these purposes central governments usually aim at maximizing gross or net foreign exchange receipts and ensuring balanced regional development. The problem of balanced regional growth again suggests that the growth of the individual tourist areas proceed at a relatively even rate and such a policy again could lead to an efficient environmental protection in the tourist areas. Such an approach to an environment/tourism policy would imply also, in certain countries, long-term nation wide tourism development planning, taking into account the environmental implications of such policies.

The discussion developed above suggests that the long-term profit maximizing principle, a rational economic behaviour on the part of the tourists and the pursuance of longer term economic goals on the part of governments would, to a large extent, ensure simultaneously the protection of the environment. This is not to suggest that other regulatory, etc., measures can be dispensed with. Rather the proposition is put forward that important contributions to environmental protection could be achieved by improving the efficiency of the market mechanism in tourism.

On the other hand, it can be demonstrated that the economic behaviour of the principal actors in the tourist sectors and in tourism in general could and has lead to environmental deterioration. This can be partly attributed to their short-run profit maximizing behaviour, partly to lack of knowledge and foresight and partly to the inability of the free market system to incorporate into prices the cost of environmental damage and the use of environmental resources.

b) The descriptive framework provides a picture how the operation of the tourism 'market' as it is operated today could be perceived in economic terms and its impacts on the environment. This description is a generalization to which many exceptions could be found. However, it is suggested that it is based on the observation of the present situation, and as economic generalizations, it is true on the average for a large number of areas observed.

i) The tourist usually acts on a limited amount of information which is not necessarily completely correct. His choice of tourist environment therefore, is not always in conformity with his preferences, but once there, it is almost impossible for him to change his location. There is only a limited amount of highly subjective information available to the tourist with price being the main determinant, subject to the promised environmental quality. In addition the tourist population is changing in any place fairly rapidly, and therefore, the tourist finds it difficult, if not impossible, to enforce his environmental demand in the area by withdrawing his demand for a specific tourist area. It is also often impossible for the tourist to reduce the environmental charges if any, imposed on him by behaving in an environmentally conscious manner.

ii) The producer of tourist services is usually a short-term maximizer. His behaviour, particularly if he is a non-local investor, might be described in the following way: his investment is constructed for maximum capacity or density as close to the environmentally highly valued attraction point as possible; his construction is often for high rate of depreciation and he aims for maximum utilization of his facilities. Aiming for recovering his capital quickly, maintenance expenditure is often kept to a minimum and capital gains are realized in the shortest possible time. Such an approach then often results in the quick deterioration of the physical and environmental capital. The imposition of possible environmental charges or full cost charging for local services is strongly resisted as they would add to prices to be charged on tourists and might also reduce total profits to be gained from overall tourist activities. The full exploitation of the employment market can also result in the detriment of local employees and a slower regional development than the tourism growth would otherwise generate.

iii) Local governments can pursue tourism policies which are to economic disadvantage of the region and also for the same reason environmentally undesirable. Such policies would aim at a rapid development of the region in terms of tourist numbers resulting in an insufficient supply of local services and in the influx of non-local labour for a limited period. A more gradual development on the other hand, would provide longer term employment for the local construction industry with the concurrent build-up of environmental services. On the financing side local government might be administratively and politically less demanding if the budget is balanced with a relatively low level of expenditure for local services rather than with large gross expenditure and large revenues from charges, etc. , to cover these services. The implications of the first strategy are low level of environmental protection and rapid environmental degradation.

iv) Central governments in their efforts to maximize foreign exchange receipt from tourism often resort to the policy of maximizing the number of tourists in the belief that this will also lead to the maximization of receipts. Such policy could have two consequences: again serious pressure will be placed on the environment of tourist areas for which the direct responsibility will not always rest with the central government. Secondly, if only tourist numbers are maximized no effort is made by the central government to charge for the facilities used by the tourist or for the environmental damage caused by the tourist in areas which are the responsibility of central governments, e.g. the use of roads. By omitting to collect the consumer surplus from the tourist, governments fail to maximize foreign exchange receipts and fail simultaneously to protect the environment. Similar considerations suggest that these policies could also lead to unbalanced regional development if the environmental costs are not charged to the tourist.

The discussion so far lead to a number of conclusions which could be important for tourist/environmental policies:

1. all the four actors in tourism could behave in a fashion, which appear to be rational in the short run, but in fact is not necessarily the most efficient way to achieve their objective;
2. all the four actors contribute to various degrees to the environmental degradation and consequently to a possible long run decline in tourism;
3. these considerations suggest that there is considerable scope for market oriented policy measures to reconcile environmental and economic objectives in tourism;
4. there is a need for governments to revise their own objectives in gaining maximum economic benefits from tourism and assist in the reconciliation of the aims of the different actors and the economic/environmental objectives.

THE IMPACT OF TOURISM INDUCED ENVIRONMENTAL DEGRADATION ON TOURISM

The original proposal for undertaking a tourism/environmental study within the OECD framework was based on the assertion that the rapid, and in some cases unplanned and uncontrolled, growth has already resulted in such a deterioration in the environment of certain tourist areas that either tourism growth or tourist revenues in absolute terms have already declined. This phenomenon is popularly known as "Tourism destroys tourism". Accordingly, the main objective of the OECD study was to examine the validity of this assertion on the basis of data and other quantitative and qualitative information provided in the case studies and suggest policy measures which will alleviate the worst excesses and will lead to improvement in policy making and eventually in the environment and in long-term tourist growth.

a) The coverage, the nature and economic background of the case studies provided by countries

More than half of the OECD Member countries have actively participated in the project by preparing national and individual case studies. Altogether 23 cases have been undertaken, some countries providing comparative studies of more than one area. * The quality of the studies and the quantitative information supplied in them varied considerably between countries and between regions.

The approach suggested in the guidelines to the case studies was a time-series analysis, comparing changes in tourist-pressure on the environment, in terms of tourist numbers, etc. , with changes in environmental quality, expressed in various indices. This approach was preferred to a comparative study of a number of regions using the same type of information (input) which could have yielded more incisive information, explaining comparative developments over time for the same country. Such approach was judged to be too costly but countries might like to explore this approach at some future stage. In cases when countries did undertake comparative studies the results were particularly illuminating both in terms of cause-effect relationships as well as to the success and failure of policies.

Not all the case studies attempted to answer directly the main question posed and this was partly due to the lack of information available on environment. There was considerable difficulty in describing let alone measuring in meaningful ways the nature and extent of environmental degradation. This is in a way not surprising considering the wide variety of tourist demand, the various national and regional attitudes and the variation in the areas under consideration.

The difficulties were further compounded by significant national difference in economic background and institutional differences.

i) The countries not participating in the project, at least not through the provision of case studies, were all high per capita income and industrially advanced societies with relatively well developed environmental legislation. These were in particular the Scandinavian countries, the United States, Canada and Germany. These countries were at the same time also the countries providing a high proportion of international tourists as well as inland tourists in the OECD area, and consequently, presumably, with considerable vested interest in good tourist environment. Three of them were large federal states with divided responsibilities in these fields and this would explain partly this lack of interest on the part of the federal authorities.

ii) The number of national and regional authorities involved in tourism and related environmental protection is quite considerable. They range from the Tourist Authorities proper through the various branches of the Ministry of Agriculture (forestry,

---

*   At the time of writing this report the final versions have not been received for all the case studies.

fishing), Ministry of Economic Affairs, Ministry of Culture (education), Ministry of Transport, Ministry of Interior (local governments) and Ministry of Environment. This dispersion of responsibilities while consistent with the basic functions of the various services and resources involved appears to contribute to the difficulties in decision-making. The role of environment ministries in most of the countries appear to be relatively limited. The cases where environmental authorities are intervening vigorously into tourist areas are those where industrial pollution is a clearly defined one major source pollution, e. g. where major oil spills occur.

The period under consideration can be divided into two distinct sub-periods: until the second half of 1973, a continuous and fast economic growth accompanied by similar growth in number of tourists and also a fast growth in the number of nights spent by tourists. This was accompanied by increases of similar magnitudes of receipts from tourism in real terms. From 1974 on the situation changed quite radically. First there was a negative economic growth and then a growth rate well below the early 1970 rates. Similarly the trend in tourism has changed: there was a fall in tourist numbers and real receipts in 1974 and only relatively modest increases in 1975 and 1976. During the same period there were a number of other economic and political disturbances influencing developments in tourism: in the economic field the world wide inflation and major disturbances in the foreign exchange markets have taken place; in the political field major domestic and international upheavals in the Mediterranean area occurred; again their impact for certain countries were severe.

In analysing the data on tourism and environment all these outside factors had to be discounted, and only then could a cause-effect relationship between environment and tourism be analysed. Even so a number of other major difficulties remained:

i) there were no specific instructions given to the countries as to the siting of the case studies; their preferences varied and they selected either an area they wished to investigate for development, or an area they thought was particularly relevant for the case study, or an area where particular consideration was given for the environment; consequently, it is uncertain how far the case studies are representative of the OECD countries;

ii) when one environmental factor is significantly more important than the others the multivariation caused is difficult to discount for; e. g. the attraction of sunshine versus a limited degree of water pollution;

iii) during a period of strong tourist growth minor declines are difficult to attribute to environmental factors.

b) The results of the case studies and other evidence

The information presented in this part largely came from the case studies but some additional information has also been collected from tourist literature and from news reporting. When it was possible this information has been presented separately. In some cases the information was provided in a specific quantitative way but this was not always the case and indeed the answer to the original question was sometimes left ambiguous. At this stage the names of the individual areas have been omitted.

Case studies where tourist numbers declined or changed composition due to longer-run environmental degradation:

   i) in an inland lake area, due to eutrification, there was a decline of 14% in tourist numbers versus a 7.6% decline for the State;

  ii) in a similar case of another inland lake there was a fall off of tourist arrivals of 8% compared to the State average of 4%;

 iii) for a coastal region a decline of 25% was reported for tourists coming from one single country due to pollution of the coast and beaches; however, it was suggested also that there was no evidence for significant pollution but rather the major tour operators decided to shift the tourists to more profitable areas;

  iv) sporadic outbreak of pollution, which appeared to be major health damage, lead to significant unspecified fluctuation in tourists in the vicinity of major coastal tourist cities;

   v) congestion, or high level density of tourists, produced a change in tourist population in one high density coastal area; it appears that tourists of certain income groups deserted the area, after it has reached a certain degree of density and a new, younger tourist replaced them; however, it was impossible to measure the degree of density which brings about this sort of change;

  vi) in two tourist areas examined tourist growth was relatively slow because of the lack of environmental infrastructure; in these cases the authorities managed to contain tourist growth to the growth of environmental protection measures, e.g. no building permit until sewerage treatment available.

Other tourism studies with environmental content:

   i) It has been shown that a major environmental damage has an immediate and substantial impact on tourist numbers; the Amoco Cadiz oil spill on the coast of Britany resulted in an estimated decline of 50% in tourist numbers. Similar

incidents of short-term duration have been reported on the
US coast in response to even minor oil slicks. However, in
all these cases the effects are transitional.

ii) Major decline in tourist numbers occurred in one region
following a season of water shortage and 40% price rise. In
this case the price rise was partly aimed at deterring a
surplus of tourists which in turn would have again resulted in
water shortage. The fall-off in tourist numbers was propor-
tional to the price rise.

iii) An OECD study examining a continuous but low level oil
pollution from tank washing from oil tankers in the form of
tar balls indicated zero impact on the tourist population.
However, in this case there was a continuous environmental
effort to remove tar balls from the beach.

iv) Relative tourist decline has also been noted in regions,
which have been well frequented, but because of the relative
age structure of hotels and other facilities the tourist environment has deteriorated; this phenomenon appears to be of a
cyclical nature and likely to affect most tourist areas in the
future; it is to a degree similar to urban decline and renewal
in metropolitan areas.

Given these reservations outlined at the beginning of this section
the most conclusive results were obtained in areas where there was a
single prominent environmental attraction. In these areas the
environmental degradation at the time of general tourist recession has
definitely lead to a significantly greater decline than in an environmentally highly attractive place. Another conclusion that emerged was
that when tourist density reaches a degree of saturation which is
intolerable to certain tourists, tourist numbers will not necessarily
decline but tourist revenues might fall off because of the change in the
type of tourist. There are numbers of these places, particularly
around the Mediterranean. The assertion is that these places will
become further and further degraded and urbanized.

In a number of cases it was emphasized that the decline occurred
in the number of foreign tourists; various inferences might be drawn
from this. Firstly, it could be suggested that foreign tourists with
relatively larger outlays are more conscious of the tourist environment; alternatively that they are, through their tourist organisation,
better informed; or that there are better tourist statistics concerning
foreign tourists.

Another point which emerged from the discussion is the continuous
assertion that many of the areas have reached the point of saturation.
This argument has, however, not been fully supported by data and
there is doubt about the usefulness of any of the indices as good
indicators of the limit for tourist expansion. As pointed out earlier

in this paper, and also in the case studies, thresholds are not static but dynamic concepts and the validity of these measurements particularly in the long run, is questionable.

ECONOMIC/FISCAL MEASURES TO PROTECT THE TOURIST ENVIRONMENT

A. Information requirements for better environmental management

a) In assessing the possible economic measures and the fiscal resources which might be used for environmental protection in the field of tourism it appears useful even imperative that sufficient information on revenues and expenditures is available. Already a substantial amount of various information is being collected both at the national and the local level. Some of these data, while quite useful for the investigation of certain trends, are not particularly suited for environmental policy purposes. These may be classified in the following fashion:

  i) gross foreign exchange receipts and outgoing on the basis of an internationally accepted definition;
  ii) gross revenues from or expenditure by tourists accruing to local businesses and local governments;
  iii) gross expenditures by local governments;
  iv) some expenditure by private entrepreneurs.

Both from the point of view of general policy making and also for the purpose of generating revenues for environmental expenditures it would help greatly if some of the revenue and expenditure items were further refined. *

At the national level:

- the various transport costs and transport revenues associated with the national movement of tourists;
- the import content of tourist expenditures;
- the possible repayment of foreign capital and associated earnings.

At the local level:

- local government revenues by major categories ;
- local government expenditures by major categories;
- business income generated by tourist activities;
- wages income generated by tourist activities.

_____

*   See for example Dr. O. Dalli "Aperçu pour la contribution du tourisme à l'économie nationale en Turquie", The Tourist Revue, No. 1, 1975.

b)   The more successful case studies have attempted to show local revenues and expenditures including the gap needed to be covered to finance the additional expenditures.   More importantly however, even if all this information were available there is no certainty that the calculations were carried out in such a way that they would produce the economically and environmentally desirable results.   The normal development calculations would look only at the relatively short-run costs and revenues or aim at recovering development cost in the possible shortest period without the accompanying consequences for the longer run.   At the same time it is also unlikely, judging from past experience, that the various social benefits and costs, including the environmental costs, would be included into the calculations.   There are basically three considerations for appropriate calculations: the relevant cost and revenue items, the method of calculation and in addition the national and regional considerations must also enter into the picture.   All these together would add up to a cost-benefit analysis for longer-term tourist development. *

i) to internalize environmental costs all the necessary expenditures to protect the environment should be included and in addition, depending on the circumstances, some of the residual damage costs would also have to be taken into account;** these items would have to be valued on a year by year basis, either when the damage occurred or when the expenditure was undertaken, whichever was the earlier. The possible implications of a development scheme for the neighbourhood would also have to be taken into account both in revenues and costs;

ii) the method of calculation should be a form of discounted cash flow analysis based on relatively long run estimates of cost and benefits. The length of the period would be determined by the relative life of the various investment undertaken and the period for which tourist demand forecasts could be prepared

iii) some sort of judgement based on priorities and net returns would have to be made at the national level in order to, decide on the choice of timing for the development of the different regions. Resources being limited not all developments could go ahead simultaneously and at the same rate. Choice would have to be made on the calculations described under i) and ii)

    *   This idea was raised also by J. Krippendorf in his "Kritische Beurteilung bisheriger methodischer Ansätze zur Bestimmung der Belastbarkeit von Erholungslandschaften"; The Tourist Review, 1977, No.1.
    **   a)   See also Economic Measurement of Environmental Damage; OECD, Paris, 1976.
         b)   Impact on Tourism from Oil Pollution on the Beaches in South-West Wales; OECD, 1978.

and on other criteria to decide where and how to develop
those environmental considerations which are not quantified
and valued should be included here.

B. How to finance the costs of environmental protection

a) When tourist development is carried out on the basis described
above it is possible to ensure that funds are also generated to carry out
environmental protection at the minimum of cost. There is evidence
to suggest that in many cases these calculations were not made and that
the environmental consequences as the result, were severe. There is
however, also evidence from the case studies that in a number of cases
charges and taxes* were imposed to generate revenues for environmental expenditure. Charges and taxes should be levied to the extent
that the users of these services or the generators of the damage would
compensate for the provision of the service or the protection of the
environment. In certain cases these charges are relatively easy to
establish, e. g. in the case of waste collection and disposal; but even
here it might be necessary to introduce other measures, e. g. fines
to maintain standards between collections or to reduce total cost. In
other cases the calculation of the charge could be more difficult, e. g.
when the long-term cost would have to be considered, such as sewerage
services; or when the charge should achieve a certain reduction in
demand, such as for parking places. The principles governing the
imposition of charges or taxes should be that they are the least costly
and most effective way of achieving the policy aim, that is producing the
service and protecting the environment; and as far as possible they
should be equitable. The most common forms are:

  i) per capita tourist tax: this is usually a nominal amount
      imposed through hotels, etc. , and aimed at collecting local
      revenue for services which are difficult to impose on the basis
      of use, law and order, fire protection, etc.;

 ii) local government tax is based on the value of property; this is
      a tax which is finally imposed on the tourist but the shifting of
      the tax burden will depend on the competitive situation; the tax
      might reflect, through the property value, the number of
      tourists using the lodging facility and it is also for more general
      services such as street cleaning and maintenance of the streets
      and sometimes also of sewerage services;

iii) charges for services according to use: for the water used in
      individual establishments, which again would show up in the
      prices charged to tourists; or charges for entering the beach

---

*   Pollution Charges - An Assessment, OCDE, 1976.

paid directly by the tourist each time of use; parking charges in the streets; local information service;

iv) other fees and licences or taxes: fishing licence, hunting licence, betting taxes, gambling fees;

v) special tolls on the use of roads and bridges.

The totality of these taxes, charges, etc. , would go toward covering expenditures in certain fields if the charge is at the 'right' level, e. g. for waste collection, water supply. They would have a direct deterring effect, e. g. to reduce congestion through parking fees and indirect effect through reducing marginally the total number of tourists.

b)   Clearly there are certain types of environmental damage which cannot be effectively avoided through the imposition of charges: charges might be insufficient to avoid the development of a region to a level which from the national point of view is regarded as undesirable.   In such cases regulations are clearly more efficient.   Similarly the consideration applies to a behaviour resulting in serious health risk, e. g. discharge of raw sewerage onto beach areas.   On the basis of similar type reasoning it was found more efficient to impose a complete ban on motor cars rather than to use high entry charges in some towns.

c)   Central governments can and should pay an important role in financing environmental expenditures.   There are two major areas of operations available to them: they themselves can collect various charges and allocate them to local governments for environmental purposes or spend the money themselves on the environment.   Alternatively they can allocate monies from the General Budget to local authorities.

i) Central governments can increase their foreign exchange receipts by charging for services rendered or for environmental damage caused:
  - charging for nationally provided services, e. g. motorways, airports;
  - charging in areas where local governments have no financing powers;
  Such policies would have to take into account other international obligations as well as the possible impact of such measures in the various regions within the country, in certain cases will also lead to a decline in the number of tourists.

ii) Within the OECD there are large variations in the revenue raising powers and the environmental obligations of central and local governments; there are however, certain similarities;
  - the infrastructure requirements of touristic areas are not covered by the 'normal' type of revenue sharing arrangements between these authorities;   some governments have

already recognized the problem of multifold increase in
population during holiday periods and try to compensate
tourist regions;
- environmental legislations are more geared to deal with
industrialized urban areas and therefore, specific needs
are not always recognized and standards might be too low
considering the specific needs of tourists or the sensitivity
of these areas.

The case studies demonstrate that the local authorities are fully
aware of the financing problem which is largely the outcome of fast
development and of the peak periods created by the tourist season,
however, the capital costs associated with peak periods cannot be
financed by the local population under the existing financing arrangements with central governments. The environmental deterioration in
many aspects is the direct outcome of this and is inevitable. The
imposition of charges in some areas helped to correct the situation to
a certain degree. The reluctance of local authorities to impose such
charges is due to the fear of loss of tourists to other areas. An international recognition of the validity of these charges and the encourage-
ment by central governments of the imposition of such charges would
induce local governments to follow such policies. In some cases it
might be necessary to give local governments additional revenue raising
powers to be able to exploit fully the financing avenues in the tourist
field.

C. How to protect the environment and improve the operation of the
tourist market

From the environmental point of view considerable gains could be
obtained from improving the market through the dissemination of the
appropriate information. With the help of such additional information
the tourist-consumer would be able to make better choices and thereby
force the protection and improvements. Similarly on the production
side better products could be provided either through increased competition and better knowledge of governmental plans.

i) Improving the environment through consumer demand for
better environment:
- education of the tourist concerning the environment which
would be advantageous from the point of view of health,
recreation, cultural enlightenment, etc. This type of
information might be provided through school education,
governmental programmes or in tourist literature;
- information concerning the environment the tourist is
buying: tourist resorts to be classified according to internationally agreed environmental criteria which are period-
ically monitored by the appropriate authorities; this

65

information is to be made available to tourists in writing
with some guarantee by the tourist or local authorities that
these conditions will be fulfilled;

- educating the tourist of his expected behaviour concerning
the environment; all international tourists to be provided
at the frontier with environmental guidelines (this sort of
information is already provided for visitors entering
national parks and similar environmentally sensitive
regions); tourist behaviour could be also included into
school curriculum or governmental adult education programmes; (recently the Federal Press and Information
Office of the German Government placed advertisements
in German magazines advising German nationals on their
behaviour during their foreign holidays).

ii) On the side of providing tourist services the environment
might be promoted also through better competition:

- private entrepreneurs should be informed of long term
tourist development plans of the government and also of
the environmental requirements in these areas; at the
same time it is also essential that speculations using
environmental requirements in certain areas are pre-
empted; speculative growth based on quick capital gains
are often environmentally poorly conceived and executed;

- exclusive rights for tourist development or monopolistic
franchise in providing services should be accompanied by
appropriate environmental safeguards; while on the one
hand it is easier to deal with a single developer than a
large number of small operators, there were examples in
the past that the large operator could disregard a small
local government.

D. How to reduce environmental cost by managing demand

The main environmental problems arise from tourism because of
peak demand, either during the weekend or holiday period or the
combination of both. These peak demands are further accentuated by
unusual weather conditions in any one country or continent or major
environmental problems such as the Amoco Cadiz or political changes
in any one major tourist country which would shift a significant number
of tourists to already over-crowded areas. While it is almost impossible to deal with the accidental type of peak demand, certain economic
measures are possible and have been taken to deal with the weekend
and holiday peaks.

During holiday peaks the population of holiday regions examined
in the case studies rose between 10-100 times. Consequently, the
capacity of the services to provide health and environmental protection

would have to rise proportionately. This applies in particular to
water supply, sewerage, road and parking facilities provided by local
governments. Similarly, a number of private capital facilities in
particular hotel accommodation and related facilities are built for peak
capacity. Reduced peak demand, which stretches over longer holiday
periods and in some cases eliminating week-end demand would reduce
cost both public and private and increase the rate of return on all
investment. There will be little saving in running cost but longer
period of local employment would result.

The environmental benefits would be substantial:

a) because of lower capital cost more protection could be provided;
b) the pressure on the environmental services at any one time
    would be less;
c) tourist and traffic density would be reduced.

The barriers to reduce peak demand are partly environmental
(climatic) and partly institutional (school holidays). On the economic
side there are already substantial incentives in terms of lower fares,
accommodation as well as in some cases, extra holidays. Because
of the substantial environmental benefits which would be generated and
the resulting improvement in welfare governments should support the
market provided incentives. The possible inconvenience due to the
change and the possible climatic losses would be compensated by the
environmental improvements. Case studies dealing with winter and
summer holidays have emphasized the problem of peak demand but
none of them demonstrated the effectiveness of measures to deal with
the problem.

Conclusions

a) There is enough evidence to support the assertion that 'tourism
destroys tourism' in certain specific regions; these effects are most
noticeable at the time of economic recession and could lead to the
development of depressed tourist regions just as much as the development of depressed industrial regions.

b) There is a large armoury of economic measures which have
been used and can be used both to improve the environment and the
tourist sector itself. These economic measures should be employed
side by side with regulations and with long-term land-use policy.

c) Through the proposed charges, taxes, etc. , governments
can increase their foreign exchange receipts, regional incomes and
will be able to finance environmental expenditures.

d)   By helping to improve the operation of the market, governments can induce the tourists to contribute to better environment and obtain better services.

e)   Peak tourist demand is the major cause of the need for expensive environmental services;   market incentives to reduce peak demand should be assisted by governments;   the environmental pay-offs are substantial.

Annex

Australia   :   National Report: Australia

Impact of Tourism on the Environment: Heron Island

Austria   :   National Report: Austria

Case Studies: Millstatter and Weissensee (Carinthia, Austria)

Case Study: Neusiedler See (Burgenland, Austria)

Canada   :   National Report: Canada
Environmental Consequences of Tourism

Spain   :   Outline of the National Report on Consequences of Tourism on the Environment

Case Study: The Huelva Coast

Case Study: Alcudia, Majorca

Case Study: Palma, Majorca

France   :   Case Studies of a Coastal Resort: Saint-Hilaire de Riez
and of a Winter Sports Resort: Montchavin (Savoie)

Comparative Study of Two Tourist Resorts: Saint-Hilaire de Riez and Montchavin

Greece   :   National Report: National Planning in the Sector of Tourism in Greece

Case Study: Patmos

Italy   :   National Report: Italy
Environment and Tourism

Case Study: The Po Delta – Quality of Environment and Tourism Exploitation

Japan	:	National Report: Japan Environmental Consequences of Tourism
		Case Study: Shiga Highland, Japan
New Zealand	:	National Report: New Zealand Environmental Consequences of Tourism
		Case Study: Queenstown
		Case Study: Bay of Islands
Netherlands	:	National Report: Netherlands Environment and Tourism
		Case Study: The Grevelingen Basin
Portugal	:	Case Study: Alvor Estuary
Switzerland	:	The Growth of Ski-Tourism and Environmental Stress in Switzerland
Turkey	:	National Report on Tourism
		Case Study: Kusadasi
		Case Study: Bodrum

III

POLICY MEASURES TO PROTECT THE ENVIRONMENT IN TOURIST AREAS AND THEIR EFFECTIVENESS*

INTRODUCTION

It seems easy enough to draw up a record of protective measures in tourist areas, but this record must be sufficiently exhaustive or, at any rate, its constituents sufficiently comparable. In any case, measuring their effectiveness is bound to be a gamble since it is precisely because of the seriousness of the unsolved problems of protection that the Group of Experts was formed.

This paper would therefore be failing in its purpose if it were not essentially critical, especially in view of the remarkable degree of understatement - or even, in some cases, overstatement - to be found in several of the reports or case studies to hand.

But despite the fact that the reports tend to be relatively guarded in what they say, I shall attempt to describe the situation in Member countries, discussing first of all the different measures adopted those countries, then the circumstances of their application and their effectiveness.

THE SITUATION AS REGARDS MEANS OF PROTECTION

A. With regard to the policy measures adopted by Member countries, most of the reports mention first and foremost the drawing up of general land-use plans and programmes, then measures concerned with different ways of developing tourism and finally measures for protecting the environment.

a) General planning measures

Many countries draw up national or regional master plans that centre on tourism or incorporate it: Turkey (as in the case of Kusadsi), Spain (Alcudia), France (schemes for coastal regions and mountain areas), New Zealand (legislation on urban and rural planning), the Netherlands (development plans like Aqua Delta), and so on. In the best of cases, these plans are carried out. But problems and solutions

---

* J.-L. Michaud, Tourism Directorate, Ministry of Youth, Sport and Recreation, Paris.

71

evolve very rapidly in this field, which in each country is the responsibility of numerous administrative departments that are not really comparable from one country to the next.

The planning instruments are for the most part devised in relation to a set of activities and not just to tourism.

At local level, the measures most frequently taken concern either the creation of natural parks and reserves or the control of urbanization New Zealand (Act of 1972), Canada, Japan (27 national parks, 50 assimilated parks, 289 prefectural parks), Great Britain (National Trust), France (national parks, regional parks) and other countries, too, have created these precincts, which are closed or open to the public depending on whether their primary purpose is to protect nature or to provide a setting for leisure activities.

Some countries, aware that space is in short supply and needs to be put to a variety of uses (Japan and France, for example) have developed the two types of parks concurrently. Others, like Canada, while differentiating between federal and provincial parks, are seeking to get open-air leisure activities into the parks: physical planning presupposes the spatial organisation of activities that are currently scattered about, just as much as their supervision.

Finally, other countries like Spain or Italy mention the weaknesses in their tourism planning arrangements: the Italian report, on the other hand, with a great deal of frankness and a courage that should be saluted, points out the deficiencies in its planning and protection procedures. This simply gives more weight to the positive observations made in the report, as for instance those concerning the measures for coastal area development in depth.

It is indeed generally proving extremely difficult to bar building completely in a very attractive region: it is preferable to channel tourist pressure and establish legal and financial procedures to enable local authorities, with assistance provided at the provincial or national level, to carry out the kind of development that is in line with the policy advocated.

b) The approaches to tourism development are seen to differ markedly from country to country. Very broadly, I would say that countries fall into three groups:

- Those which have a long-standing tradition of tourism, and the development of whose tourism infrastructures, like relations with the other sectors of activity, has harmonized naturally with the geographical, economic and socio-cultural characteristics of the regions concerned; this is the case, in particular, with the region in which we are at present and, more broadly,

with the whole of Austria, where there is a question of adjusting
the size of local districts the better to accommodate the new
dimensions of tourism.

- Those countries which, having recently experienced a large-
  scale development of tourism, especially in areas sparsely
  populated hitherto, sought to attract investment and tourist
  business by producing the industrial tourism "model" of the
  1960s, with heavy concentration and mass building. * These
  countries are now ill-equipped to control the influx of tourism,
  speculative real estate booms, internationalization of profits
  and the spread of stereotyped building.
- Finally, there are those which succumbed to the charms of that
  approach for a while but very soon encountered the excesses
  which it permits when the custom catchment areas are close by
  (France, Italy and Spain). To varying degrees, they are now
  trying to adapt the actual characteristics of tourism development to regional and local possibilities: those countries,
  because of their highly mixed nature (strong tourist-generating
  potential, large receptive capacity), seem to be the most
  threatened. This explains why France, for example, has
  recently redefined its national policy in this area (see the
  report "Choisir ses loisirs").

So the fact is that the majority of Member countries, though they
have certain physical planning instruments and - as we shall see in a
moment - a great many means of protecting the environment, have
very little in the way of a real tourism development strategy with an
environmental character.

   c)   As for environmental protection measures, there are a very
great many. It would be tedious to go over them all, ranging as they
do from protection of the cultural and historical heritage to preservation
of landscapes and control of pollution and disamenities. Even so, we
find that many countries (Japan being one of them) present us with
intentions more than achievements. Others, by limiting their investigations to one particular aspect or region, make it impossible to draw up
any overall record of environmental protection measures. Moreover,
such a record has to be drawn up on a country-by-country basis and in
the light of actual achievements.

B.   Conditions of application and effectiveness of protective measures

   Generally speaking, the measures whose effectiveness it is possible to assess are those which have already been in operation for a
number of years. Since in most Member countries tourism has only
recently achieved a scale or intensity that necessitate environmental

---

   *   Hotels, secondary residences, holiday villages.

controls, most of the protective measures already in force were actually devised for other reasons (control of continuing urbanization, industrial pollution, etc.).

The effects of these protective measures are by definition not very conspicuous since their aim in principle is to prevent damage to the environment, and only if this fails, to repair it. It is only in extreme situations where a deteriorated environment has to be improved (whether for a reason connected with tourism or not) that it is possible to gauge the effects which reparative measures may have on tourism activity. And even then, though it was possible, for example, to estimate the loss of tourist business in Brittani as a result of the Amoco Cadiz oil spill at Frs. 800 million in 1978, how can one put an exact value on the effect of the huge clean-up operation that was carried out before August?

The problems of how to calculate the effectiveness of measures are, as we all know, very complex. First of all, because these effects have to be measured not only on a local scale but also on a regional or national scale; not only in the economic context, but also from the social standpoint; not only in the tourism sector as such, but also in terms of quantity and quality of the leisure activities of the inhabitants (who obviously are going to want a region with an attractive environment); and not only for the short term but also for the long.

So it seems more practical to determine whether the measures and their application have met the policymakers' aims both from the standpoint of protection of the environment and from that of the continuing development of tourism.

In this regard, some of the country reports and case studies are more explicit than others. Each country considers on the one hand that application of the measures is not complete and on the other that they cannot be immediately effective. What is more, in cases of excessive coastal pollution, let us say, a lot of governments do not hesitate to put the health of tourists in danger by authorizing bathing before the effects of possible cleansing operations have been clearly established.

Member countries' efforts have in fact tended in three directions:

i) Spatial planning and control of spontaneous building development (continuing concentrated urbanization of coastal areas, uncontrolled building-up of rural and mountain areas). It seems in this connection that the effectiveness of the measures varies considerably from country to country, with - as far as can be judged from the reports - definite efforts in the Netherlands, for example, and much less evident efforts in Italy and Spain except on the Atlantic coast (e. g. Alcudia). It should be noted here that because of this difficulty in ensuring observance of planning regulations, Italy is planning to tax secondary residences.

ii) Adaptation of the features of tourism development to local possibilities. The aim of policymakers here seems to be achieved when continuing expansion of tourism activity does not harm the local environment because:

- new building styles have been made to blend with earlier architecture;
- investment and management of tourism have been brought under control by local economic transactors (small or medium-sized hotel businesses, rented accommodation);
- certain socio-cultural values which constitute the distinctiveness of the area have been respected.

In other words, it seems that choice of the right scale is essential to the effectiveness of action to control tourism, since it facilitates compliance with the physical, economic and socio-cultural tolerance levels of the environment.

iii) Thirdly, measures to protect the environment are, of course, the easiest to measure as to their effectiveness.

Environmental protection of tourist regions usually rests on general regulatory and financial procedures (tax on effluents in the Netherlands or France, for example) which are applied to tourism where necessary.

In these circumstances their effectiveness is naturally limited by the specific features of tourist activity. Thus the communication and sanitation infrastructures in tourist regions are hardly sufficient (at any rate in coastal areas) to cope with the influx of visitors in peak periods, when the population in the most frequented areas may increase as much as tenfold.

THE SIX PARADOXES OF ENVIRONMENT-ORIENTED TOURISM POLICIES

The keynote of this summary presentation is very naturally one of contradiction and paradox. After all, tourism and environment reports are by nature contradictory and paradoxical.

a) The first conclusion, which will partly explain the weakness of those that follow, is that while that the tourist phenomenon has developed at an extraordinary pace over the last twenty years, it is equally extraordinary that knowledge of this phenomenon should have failed so singularly to progress. Admittedly, enterprises have developed numerous special techniques (management, marketing, promotion, reservation, etc.), but understanding of the global aspects of tourism and how its components interact has scarcely advanced.

This is especially true of the relationship between tourism and the environment.

The cause would appear to lie both in the area of policy-making and in that of science:

- From the policy standpoint, very few government and administrative officials have grasped both the economic role of tourism in its true dimensions and the absolute necessity of protecting the environment.
- From the scientific standpoint, knowledge of tourism, just like that of the environment, presupposes research of an interdisciplinary nature, which is all the less developed in that tourism and the environment are recent science subjects.

b)   The second conclusion is not unrelated to the first; the profusion of information about tourist resources is paralleled only by its lack of credibility. This is partly due to the promotional nature of the information put out by official organisations, anxious to paint an attractive picture of the tourist areas which they are responsible for putting on the map. It is quite obvious, despite the concern with objectivity revealed in many reports, that this consideration shows in the national assessments or case studies.

c)   The third conclusion is still more paradoxical; it is the countries most affected by the surge of tourism which are least equipped to control its effects on the environment. This can be explained as follows:

- the countries of Northern Europe as a whole, which became industrialized and urbanized earlier, have a tradition of physical planning and in many cases actual government departments responsible for the environment. In addition, tourism is of secondary importance for these countries: so the problem of accommodating it in their policies is less acute and better managed;
- the Mediterranean countries, on the other hand, have only very recently become aware of the problems of protecting the environment from the inroads of tourism, which is itself recent and represents a major source of income; only in a very few cases do these countries have the relevant administrative bodies and legislation;
- the non-European Member countries lie at various points between these two extremes.

d)   This observation explains a fourth paradox. It is the tourism authorities who are anxious, much more than the environmental services, for where the environmental departments are large the problem is not and, conversely, where the problem is acute the environmental bodies are small and lack resources. There are admittedly, a few exceptions - such as France, which is in an intermediate position, being a country with an industrial tradition and at the same a tourist country; in this case, even if the instruments (administrative and regulatory) for protecting the environment exist, they are not necessarily sufficient to control the tourist influx.

e)   The reason why there is often a discrepancy between policies and results is also somewhat paradoxical. In most Member countries - more so of course in the centrally planned economies, and to a lesser degree in the federally organised countries - it is at national level that awareness is greatest and that policies are framed and measures decided. However, their actual implementation usually rests with local authorities, whose grasp of environmental problems is slight, whereas their immediate interest in the continuing development of tourism is considerable.

f)   A sixth contradiction stems from the other five: the anticipatory character of environmental protection policies is seen to be limited - and their operational scope still more so - whereas the damage done to the environment is irreversible, unlike damage in the economic and social spheres, for example. Thus, it is in an area where policies need to be very forward-looking that they appear to be particularly short-sighted in the majority of cases. Let us hope that this seminar will be sufficiently thought-provoking and its conclusions sufficiently publicized for the vital process of awakening to gather momentum.

CONCLUSIONS

By way of conclusion I would emphasize that the effectiveness of protection policies is all the more lasting - even though, of course, it is still very difficult to gauge exactly - if the effort is made upstream of the development process.

So the best possible approach is to devise and apply overall spatial planning that incorporates the tourism element and control it preventively. Planning of this kind has the advantage of maximum effectiveness over the long term if it is applied in a sustained manner. On the other hand it has the disadvantage of being difficult to implement rapidly and integrally.

An intermediate level of effectiveness is attained by trying to adapt the specific characteristics of tourism schemes to the local environment. This strategy, which serves as a back-up to development, is easier to implement and does offer a satisfactory degree of effectiveness.

A policy that constitutes a bare minimum is to adopt specific measures to control pollution and safeguard the countryside. Although relatively easy to apply and quickly perceptible in their effects because of their highly specific and partial nature, such measures have an essentially curative function.

These three types of intervention are, in practice, closely complementary and it is difficult to see why, given that more and more people are becoming environment-minded, governments, for reasons of economic policy as well as social policy, should not make use of them simultaneously.

IV

THE NEED FOR POLICY ACTION [*]

INTRODUCTION

Aims of the paper

The purpose of this paper is to define concisely and to bring together, some of the types of policies which appear to be necessary, and whose implementation is required, if we are to reconcile tourism-development, with the protection and conservation of our environment. In particular, attention is given to institutional, economic and social aspects of this question, and reference is made to the international, national, and sub-national levels of action. Indication is given of some of the international interest and efforts made within this field, and to some of the areas of progress.

For purposes of this paper, one may crudely divide the international community into three types of country:

a) Developed countries which display a mixed response to international tourism, though usually having a strongly developed focus on resident recreation and even upon domestic tourism.

b) Developing countries again mixed in response to international tourism, but very often seeing it as a crude panacea for solving domestic economic problems.

c) Developing countries, at an intermediate stage, which had an early entry into international tourism (e. g. Spain), and are already into a remedial phase of action in relation to those areas which were extensively developed by tourism.

Assumptions

Important starting assumptions are made in this field, without all the supporting evidence being presented, namely:

---

[*] A.S. Travis, University of Birmingham.

a)   That international tourism is an industry of great economic significance.   For many nations international tourism represents a favourable balance of trade to the home country.   Some countries (e. g. the Netherlands) have an imbalance of trade in tourism movements, and may have strong lobbies against 'excessive' tourism to their countries by external visitors.   Tourism depends upon coherent planning, management and marketing at levels that range from the international, via the national and regional to the local scale.

b)   That tourism's long term perspective must of necessity interrelate appropriate development with the conservation of three critical sets of tourism-resources:

- the maintenance of a high quality of natural resources of air, land, and water, of clear light, sun, favourable climate and weather characteristics;
- protecting the integrity of the man-made resources of the built heritage of historic cities, towns, townscape, sites, buildings and relics - (archaelogical, historic, architectural, etc.);
- protecting and enhancing the cultural resources of society, the associations, values, identity, artistic and cultural character, cultural activities and heritage.

c)   That the foregoing resources give rise to the desirable differences in character of places, which, as a generator of tourist activity, must be maintained.   Tourism, like urbanization and industrialization - (with which it has associations) is a user of resources, can be a resource-destroyer and is a generator of infrastructure, facilities, and activities.   Thus its impacts, benefits and losses require to be evaluated, in advance of development.

d)   That whilst legitimate locational differences may require to be maintained, the achievement of similar minimal standards and safeguards may require to be defined and achieved - both in the short term interests of the tourists, and in the long term interests of the host society which provides the host environment for them.

Review of data sources

This paper's contents are based upon some three primary sources of data:

a)   That contained within the material produced for over forty major international conferences held, and published reports which have focussed totally or partially on fundamental questions of Environmental Conservation and Tourism Development.   These are listed in Appendix I to this paper, from which it can be seen that extensive involvement has been at all levels of Government, and by many types of agency.

b) Some of that data which has been produced in connection with the current series of Conferences, discussions and research activities sponsored by the OECD's Environment Directorate in Paris.

c) The primary data which has been gathered by the writer in connection with his own research work conducted in some ten countries, in four of which data collection, collation and evaluation has been in considerable detail. Reference is made in Appendix II to some of the secondary data sources which have been drawn upon.

LONG-TERM VERSUS SHORT-TERM

Long-term benefits versus short-term benefits

a) Taking actions which ensure the <u>long-term maintenance</u> of <u>tourism resources</u>, (be they natural or man-made) is good economics, as it can mean long-term economic returns from their use.

b) <u>Use-saturation</u>, damage to, or destruction of resources, means short-term rip-offs, and long-term disbenefits.

c) <u>Joint action</u> on shared environmental resources, can safeguard long-term gains to all concerned - e.g., to groups of nations surrounding one sea, or one lake, or sharing between them: one river system.

d) The principle of <u>maximizing long-term</u> income to regions and to nations, makes better economic sense than maximizing numbers of tourists. Systematic long-term planning of the economy and of the environment aids this process.

e) It is postulated that bio-social resource-based approaches to tourism are the best long-term economic approach. Thus the ecological systems provide frameworks within which economic and physical planning and management may take place.

The need to relate short-term actions to long-term policies

a) The current <u>economic recession</u> is one of the reasons why action is being concentrated in this field: current competition for trade is great, because of the potential economic benefits from success in it.

b) <u>Tourism</u> already ranges from being the first, to the fourth <u>largest industrial sector</u> in terms of value in several national economies.

c)   Enforced drops in public spending in some sectors of national economies has led to more use of mixed public/private programmes: tourism lends itself to small public trigger investments, attracting private sector responses, and having significant multiplier effects.

d)   Tourism is an internationally 'traded' commodity: a substantial proportion of tourist industry being international. The industry gives rise to national gains, aiding the balance of payments, earning hard currency, etc. However, the long-term view requires that the interests of domestic tourism, as well as of international tourism be met. Furthermore, the economic benefits arising from commercial tourism, must be balanced with the social needs and social benefits arising from 'social tourism'.

e)   Protecting the vested economic interests of nation states, is behind tourist-related programmes of nationally-owned airlines, shipping lines, national rail systems, national toll-motorway systems, state hotel and other service interests.

f)   In the past crisis-measures taken in response to sudden tragedies, teach us economic lessons, e. g. the loss of tourist income to coastal regions (Brittany Cornwall, etc.) after oil pollution, loss of mountain region income after an epidemic scare in a mountain resort, news of flood damage to island and lowland tourist regions, etc.

g)   Short-term remedial action pays off: damage to the environment builds up quickly and has cumulative effects.

h)   Increasingly short-term investment in tourism-area development and resort development, is seen as a key element in a process of regional development and regional planning.

The need to define and safeguard critical resources for tourism

a)   For any given territory the set of resources needs first to be recognized, defined, inventoried and then effectively protected. Biotic resources and cultural resources - easily placed at risk in developing economies, represent long-term economic resources for those societies and must be protected and managed, in consequence. Equally, there must be a 'fit' or safeguard for a comparable quality of life for resident populations with that of visitor-populations, if tourism is to have the off-given 'neo-colonial' and 'inequitable' tags removed from it, particularly where relatively poor developing countries act as host to visitors from richer lands. Direct economic feedbacks to the local and regional economy are critical requirements. The host-population and local services are important in themselves, and, are incidentally basic resources in relation to tourism.

b)   Maintaining the high quality of environmental resources, or restoring the quality of freshwater and seawater resources, dealing with air pollution, of damage or threats to flora and fauna, conserving the integrity of the built-environment, and of the cultural environments - represents a set of safeguarding actions critical to the continuing development of tourism.   Some advanced countries like the USA, Netherlands and Denmark, may put extensive resources into outdoor recreation provisions.   These are for use by residents and domestic tourists.   Recreation-resources are also usable as tourism-resources, if their nature, scale, character and capacity permit it.   Recreational needs and domestic tourism needs of the home population must be safeguarded as a primary requirement.

c)   Over and above the 'tourism resources' defined earlier in this paper, is the complementary provision of tourist facilities to cover needs of tourists for sleeping accommodation, for eating, resting, travel, for play, for health and hygiene, for safety, convenience and comfort.   These needs are met through the planning, development, management and maintenance of tourism-infrastructure (roads, piped and wired services, etc.) and superstructure (the buildings, sites and plants for services).

d)   Just as tourism facilities may be developed from scratch, so may limited tourist resources be expanded and supplemented:

- e. g. , social use of natural environment resources may be 'increased' by adding to the number and extent of national parks and nature reserves, complete with all the necessary protective measures in a nation-state.   The provision of national parks and nature reserves is still of a nominal order in many countries, getting low political and funding priorities; some countries (e. g. the UK) have no national parks which meet the IUCN criteria; forest resources may be added to by large-scale afforestation, and water resources both conserved by recycling and water areas added to by dam and reservoir construction, controlled flooding and after-use of quarries, sand and gravel pits.   In developing countries, the stage and state of development values, and culture may inhibit wildlife conservation.   If conservation constrains life-supporting hunting and other rural economic activities, not only resultant compensatory budgetary allocations, but legitimate economic alternatives must be made available to the affected human sub-populations;
- e. g. , built environment heritage resources may gain from pedestrianisation schemes which rapidly increase the use area of safe, clean and multi-use areas in urban centres; conservation and facelift schemes may increase not only the quantity,

but raise the quality of historic cities, quarters, sites and buildings available for use for new functions and activities. Increasing the length of stay in city centres, boosting environmental quality and experience, enhances the tourist experience;

- e. g. , cultural heritage resources may be expanded by action programmes, subsidies, provision of facilities to cultural and artistic groups - be they professional or amateur. Active nurturing of folk/naive/primitive traditions in dance, music, costume, cuisine, art, building - are economically justified in the long-term.

INSTITUTIONS AND POLICIES

Recognition of the 'actors' and of the institutions in tourism-planning

a)   Reference has already been made to all the levels at which action is taken on inventorising, and planning tourist resources. Leaving the international scale aside, momentarily, who are the key actors, and what roles do they play nationally and internationally?

- nationally there are the Public Sector actors, who have the roles of defining, providing for, planning, and guaranteeing tourism, plus that of safeguarding tourist interests and host interests.
  National Government, its Ministeries and agencies, linked to regional and local government bodies usually play these roles;
- nationally and internationally, are the Private Sector actors whose primary roles are in selling tourist services, and often providing at least a part of the tourism facilities.
  (Airline/shipping/hotel/catering interests/travel agents/tour operators/developers/investors/commercial groups and farmers may be included).

Fundamental to all the resources, facilities and services, are the assumptions we make about the nature of the tourist experience. An emergent 'sociology of tourism' now provides crude alternative explanations of this experience, ranging from the early views of Clawson and Huizinga, to the latter ones of MacCannell, and Cohen, and of Kaplan. Those involved in planning and managing the tourist industry, require to reconcile not only costs and benefits, but also conflicting assumptions made in writings on the sociology of tourism, versus these countings on the economics of tourism.

- Nationally and internationally, key actors are the tourists who may be defined as generators of demands, consumers of tourist services/facilities and users of tourist resources. Reference has already been made to the 'tourist experience' or tourism phenomenon. The Voluntary Sector often also plays a key role in provision, promotion, protection and conservation.

b)   From evidence given in sources (Appendix I), it is clear that there is not one style, but many styles of tourism-planning. This activity must always fit into and reflect the socio-economic, cultural and political conditions of each country. Inevitably, with variations in political systems, stage of development, power structures, and degrees of centralization, the range is an extensive one.

c)   Similarly a range of institutions is needed to plan, guide, develop, manage and conserve the tourism developments and tourism resources. Generally these institutions are in the public sector, and include Government Ministries of Tourism, Planning, Environment, Culture, etc. , and tourist organisations such as Development corporations, Companies, etc. , plus nature conservation and heritage built-environment conservation agencies. The institutions define the policies which address issues such as those raised earlier.

The several types of policies needed by the institutions

These include:

a)   Physical development policies which utilize land-use, i. e. spatial and activity zoning, density, capacity and design control factors. Policies on the protection of air, water-quality and safeguarding public health standards are basic in the physical environmental realm. As evidenced in contrasting situations around the Mediterranean, one cannot take the implementation of such policies for granted.

b)   Policies on access and inaccessibility, transport-planning relating the location and optimum capacity of tourism developments, to their accessibility by transportation, and the designation and protection of related sensitive heritage resources, which may be protected in part by their planned inaccessibility.

c)   Economic policies including those of an aspatial kind suggested by OECD and EEC plus spatial development policies of an enabling kind, controls and economic deterrent-actions, remedial action-policies and peripheral or development-area policies. Taxes, fines, grants and loan policies.

d)   Conservation - planning policies (such as those promoted by IUCN) to protect and manage natural heritage resources, to maintain their character and quality.

e) Cultural and educational policies relating to activity, behaviour, interpretation, learning and understanding of the urban and rural environments, and of social and cultural heritage, with grant support measures (aside UNESCO, ICOMOS and Council of Europe suggestions).

It is the complex inter-action of these sets of policies, that may comprise the system of policy-planning for tourism and the environment.

The policy fields for which standards and norms are required

It follows from what has already been said, that there is in consequence a range of policy fields for which standards and norms are required. Whilst in developed countries physical planning standards may wrongly be taken for granted, there is nevertheless often neglect of:

a) Standards of environmental quality: such as acceptable noise-levels, and minimal standards of air quality, of water quality and essential levels of life within sea and freshwater environments, actions for safeguarding standards of biotic output of certain critical types of ecosystem (e. g. estuarine zones), design standards, and controls of advertising displays in town and country, dumping, wastes, tipping, standards and frequency of street cleaning and refuse removal, and its treatment, etc.

b) Consumer protection standards in terms of public health, hygiene and cleanliness, food, restaurant and water quality monitoring. Norms for overcrowding of hotels, camping and caravan sites and essential provisions in a range of types of tourist development. Consumer protection in relation to consumer services to tourists.

CRITERIA, PRINCIPLES AND SAFEGUARDS

Criteria and principles to guide the 'providers' or 'managers' in tourism

Thus it follows that principles to guide the 'providers of tourism' include:

a) That planning must be for the increased and long-term economic wellbeing of the host community, using tourist development to bring those desirable physical and economic changes it wants for itself. Conflicts between national and regional versus local interests in this optimisation process, require resolution via advance-planning.

b)   That raising of health, hygiene and environmental standards gives benefits both to the host community and to the visitors, and generates longer-term gains in tourism.

c)   That the general principle that the polluter pays (ppp) is a sound one in economic and environmental benefit terms; but this principle has notable limitations, for if the pollution, or change process creates irremedial harm, or irreversible change, paying does not help.

d)   That a destroyed tourist resource may thus be irreplaceable, regardless of cost, therefore there is a need to establish the principle of assessing the impact gains and losses of a potential development, before accepting or rejecting a proposal for tourist development.

e)   The principle of ensuring the effectiveness of tourist expenditure, and satisfaction is particularly important - because of the high expectations of the holiday tourist, of his tourist experience, and because of the economic gain to the host community of repeat-visits. Sociological and perceptual psychology literature gives us further evidence in this realm.   As little as is known about holiday tourist perceptions, we apparently know even less in respect of business tourism, and educational tourism.

Safeguards for the tourists as 'users' of tourist resources

Commercial tourism and social tourism give rise to a range of necessary safeguards:

a)   The Integrity of tourism resources must be ensured, if generations of tourists are to experience the nature of a particular place, and not just experience the feeling of being in a placeless crowd.

b)   The tourist expects the tourist location to give improved health and refreshment, and not put his health at risk, because of poor health safeguards.

c)   Personal safety and security of the travelling or visiting tourist from attack, criminal and civil disorders, malpractices, is expected.   'Dangerous countries and regions' may not fulfil their real potential for tourism.

d)   Ease and pleasantness of visits relate to host behaviour, and attitudes to visitors, natural hospitality and the responsiveness by, and responsibility of the tourists.

Action-programmes can deal with some of the two latter sets of problems specified.

RIGHT POLICIES AT THE APPROPRIATE LEVEL

Policies at the international level of action

Historically we have seen the slow move forward internationally from a stage of response to dire problems, through to one of joint stronger remedial actions by world bodies and groups of governments. The focus has been on dealing with pollution of the seas, coasts and rivers, the freer movements of people and goods, health agreements, travel and transport agreements. Appendix I contains much evidence to this effect, covering measures regarding the:

a)   Seas - like the Mediterranean, Baltic and Atlantic, for example.

b)   Rivers like the Rhine, Danube, etc.

c)   Coasts (as in the Ramoge Project for the shared coastline of 3 countries).

The coastal and estuarine zones are possibly the vital natural resources for political action in cleaning and safeguarding.

d)   Mountain-zones and conservation - relating to links between countries sharing a resource: e.g. France and Italy; Czechoslovakia and Poland; Canada and the USA; or Sweden and Norway, or even a whole alpine system -- as was the focus of the Council of Europe's Grindelwald Conference.

Increasingly, international action and measures are relating to the scale and nature of the natural system which represents the shared resource, and multiple use or reciprocal arrangements on transport, currency exchange, health coverage of visiting nationals, etc.

At the international scale, agreement is widening both upon the definition of critical resources, and of defined key problems; monitoring of changes to the resources is now starting to be undertaken. Statistical definitional differences remain a major hazard; plans and joint plan preparation relative to tourism, and to the environment is a growing activity, but the implementation and enforcement of plans - both nationally and internationally, lags behind.

Policies at the national level of action

a)   From the foregoing text it is evident that national governments can be guided by principles:

- that Government has a fundamental responsibility to protect
  and conserve heritage tourism-resources. This they may do
  in the context of the planning and conservation activities;
- that Government should concentrate on types of tourist development which generate maximum income to the nation and do
  least damage to the environment. Concern for domestic as
  well as international tourism development is essential;
- that Government must take both preventative and remedial
  actions to maintain environmental quality, and may be aided
  by the Polluter-Pays-Principle. National government should
  link protection with development of recreation, as well as
  tourist opportunities for domestic and foreign users.

b)   There is a need for government not only to draw up national
policies for economic development, physical development-planning,
and conservation-planning, but to define standards, and machinery
for achieving them via these planning and management processes.
National policies need also address problems of time or seasonal
imbalance of demand, and of space, or the locational distribution of
tourist activities across its territory.

Policies at the regional level of action

a)   Whilst national planning is concerned with broad strategies
of development and conservation, dealing with inter-regional relationships and roles, the critical level for action-planning is at the lower -
or regional planning scale.

b)   Tourism-development is a key new form of regional development. Just as in the past regional development has focussed on
industrial and office location controls and incentives, now increasingly
the vocabulary of regional planning, includes Tourism Growth Points,
Poles, Corridors. Notable recent examples are Italy's 'Tourism
Development Areas', Northern England's 'Growth-points for Tourism',
and Israel's 'Priority areas for Tourist Development'. Such plans
include economic measures, plus physical, social, and cultural elements.

c)   Regional strategies for tourism development, thus require to
be closely related to several other facet-plans, namely:

- plans for infrastructure development, land-use and transport
  plans;

89

- plans for <u>recreation and sport development</u> (for residents and visitors - home and foreign);
- plans for <u>conservation-management</u> including national parks, nature reserves, forests and game reserves, buffer and peripheral protective zones.

d)   <u>Guiding principles</u> for such development relate to the distribution of tourist movements, capacity of transport networks, positive guidelines for the extent, capacity and design character of developments, accommodation, facilities and services, and their capacity, related to the carrying capacities and maintenance of the <u>conserved heritage areas</u>. Temperate forests have relatively high visitor capacities. Respect for regional culture, aids the uses of deflection-strategies, locational magnets or 'honey-pots', and a sum of resource-management, and people-management measures available to planners and managers.

e)   Included in the range of development-planning and conservation-planning techniques relevant to this scale are the specific <u>techniques such as Input-Output Analysis</u>, <u>Threshold Analysis</u>, <u>Potential Surface Analysis</u>, <u>Planning Balance Sheet</u>, and <u>Environmental Capacity</u> and <u>Environmental Impact Studies</u>. Planning, analysis, management, and protective techniques are available for use by agencies or institutions working in this sphere.

f)   The fit of <u>supply</u> to <u>demand</u> is increasingly tying product-development to clearly identifiable segments of demand, and social need.

Policies at the local and site-levels of action

a)   A set of <u>guiding principles</u> whereby local government dealing with area-planning and management may aid tourism-development and environmental-protection, should highlight firm policies at the extremes - e.g. critical or optional development-points or <u>areas</u>, plus preservation/conservation-zones, giving some flexibility. These principles are:

- <u>to maximize on legitimate limited local opportunities for high capacity development</u>. Thus <u>cities</u>-capitals, and industrial and commercial areas as well as seaside <u>resorts</u>, mountain-resorts, and <u>spas</u> may have high capacity potential. Not only whole settlements but sites can have high physical capacity and be acceptable in terms of their cultural economic and ecological parameters too, and have the appropriate high level of accessibility;

(e. g. at the site-development scale pedestrianised, city centres, hotel and lido complexes, indoor leisure centres, conference and exhibition centres, major transport termining and theme-parks - such as Tivoli (Copenhagen), Disneyland, Madurodam (Hague), etc. , as well as major resort beaches may be included).
It should be noted that a site like Disney World - at one extreme, handles as many tourists p. a. as a city like London does foreign tourists (10 million p. a.);

- to respect and protect those areas which are sensitive to visitor-pressures, are by their nature - fragile, and have a low-user capacity.
These include scientific protection - i. e. for nature reserves, conserved ecosystems, flora, fauna, or small sites and relics of cultural, scientific, association ... for which ecological thresholds may be defined.
Some low capacity areas must be protected - to protect an experience for the user, as much as for its scientific impor-tance, e. g. a 'wilderness area' - is to protect the opportunity of human contact with wild nature, to find isolation and quiet. This thus involves 'perceptual' or 'psychological capacity' of a place. Flexible detailed-planning should thus be possible within robust general physical planning;

- to respect the 'genius loci' or feeling of a place, and enhance it by appropriate actions: e. g. , the adaptation of vernacular villages and historic buildings for appropriate tourist uses as well exemplified by the best work in Greece, Israel and Yugoslavia;

- to protect locality and place by making the polluter pay.

b)   A spectrum of local and site policies are required which may:

- draw upon use of a range of local authority services, such as those responsible for tourism planning, town planning, land-use and transport planning, public health management, and leisure-services planning. The extent of private sector involvement with them is a variable;

- these services act as providers or managers of tourism, and will jointly plan and manage tourism and conservation at the local scale - together with the private sector interests;

- the tourists, as users are involved in a range of actions which contribute to the local economy, use the environment and services: drawing upon transport, health, shopping, accom-modation, environmental interpretation, and other facilities there.

c) It is at the <u>local and site</u> levels where synthesis of all the provisions is most needed and the users responses may be most easily recognized, measured, and evaluated. This is where the impact of tourism upon the environment, and environment upon the tourist, may most effectively be discerned.

SELECTED INDICATIVE LIST OF RELEVANT INTERNATIONAL CONFERENCES, AND REPORTS RELATING TO THE SUBJECT AREA

1965 1. Conference on Tourism and Travel; Rome; (ECE) UN.

   1b. Renovation of Monuments; Vienna; Council of Europe.

1967 2. Ecology, Tourism and Recreation; Proceedings of the 10th Technical Meeting; Morges; IUCN.

   3. Protection of the Coasts of Europe; Conference; Council of Europe.

   4. Tourism Development and Economic Growth; Estoril; OECD.

   4b. Conservation and Planning; Council of Europe; The Hague.

1969 5. Convention on North Sea Anti-Oil Pollution; Bonn.

   6. Planning and Development of Recreation Areas, including the Development of the Natural Environment; New York; (ECE) UN.

   6b. UNESCO/ICOMOS and OECD; Conservation and Tourism, Oxford.

1970 7. Report of the Inter-Regional Seminar on Physical Planning for Tourist Development; Dubrovnik; UN.

1971 8. Premoli Report on Protection of Europe's Coastal Areas; Strasbourg, Council of Europe.

   9. Conference on Problems Relative to the Environment; Prague; (ECE) UN.

   10. Conference on the Changing World of (Economic) Markets; Nassau.

   11. International Meeting of Experts on the Management of the Environment; Council of Europe.

1972	12.	Conference on the Protection of World Cultural and Natural Heritage; UNESCO.
	13.	2nd World Conference on National Parks for the Future; Yellowstone (USA); (Report in 1974); IUCN.
	14.	International Conference on Tourism and the Environment; London; BTA.
	15.	World Conference on the Human Environment; Stockholm; UN.
1973	16.	International Conference on Tourism and the Environment; Glasgow; STB.
	17.	European Conference on Parks and Reserves; Paris; French Government and the Council of Europe.
	18.	Tourism and Conservation Working Together; Copenhagen; Europa Nostra and the European Travel Commission.
	19.	1st European Ministerial Conference on the Environment; Vienna; Council of Europe.
1974	20.	Conference on Tourism and the Environment in Europe; European League for Economic Co-operation.
	21.	International Seminars on Tourism Forecasts and Tourism and the Balance of Payments; London; IUTO/ BTA.
	22.	Conference on Government and the Development of Tourism, OECD.
	23.	Congress of the 8th International Tourism Exchange; Berlin; (AMK). Berlin.
1975	24.	Report on Mediterranean Study of Environmental Degradation and Pollution of Coastal Development; Paris; OECD.
	25.	International Colloquy on the Specific Problems of Renewing Plant Cover in the Mediterranean Area; Cagliari; Government of Italy and Council of Europe.
	26.	International Conference on Environmental Education in a Rural and Urban Setting; Government of Netherlands and Council of Europe.
	27.	European Technical Conference on Leisure and Nature Conservation; Hamburg; Federal Republic of Germany and Council of Europe.

28. Conference of European Ministers responsible for Sport; Brussels; Council of Europe.

29. Planning and Development of the Tourist Industry in the ECE Region; Dubrovnik; UN Economic and Social Council.

30. Conference on the Impact of Tourism; San Diego; Travel Research Association (USA).

31. Final Conference of European Architectural Heritage Year; Amsterdam; Council of Europe and Europa Nostra.

1976 32. 2nd European Ministerial Conference on the Environment; Brussels; Council of Europe.

33. Conference on Management Problems in the Sphere of Tourism; Athens; AIEST.

34. World Conference on the Human Habitat and Settlements; Vancouver; UN.

35. Conference on Planning and Development of the Tourist Industry in the OECD Region; New York; UN.

1977 36. Congress of the 11th International Tourism Exchange; Berlin; AMK.

37. Colloquy on the Conservation of Living Resources of the Seas; Malta; Council of Europe.

38. International Heritage Conference; Woburn (England); BTA.

39. Development of Tourism in Mountain Regions; Vienna; Council of Europe.

1978 40. 1st European Symposium on the Counciliation of Social and Economic Development with the Conservation of Protected Areas; Salonica; Council of Europe.

41. Symposium on Tourist Industry Development; Dubrovnik.

NOTE: Even this indicative list excludes many other, only slightly less directly relevant Conferences, Reports, etc. of UNESCO; ICOMOS; IUTO; WTO; OECD; IATA; UNCTAD; WHO; UN. Statistical Commission, etc.

Appendix II

A SELECTED LIST OF OTHER KEY RELEVANT
REPORTS AND BOOKS

1. OECD Tourism Policy + International Tourism in OECD Member
    Countries: Paris, OECD, 1976.

2. Man in the Living Management; Institute of Ecology, USA, 1972.

3. Economic Impact of Tourism in Developing Countries; Sadler and
    Archer, Bangor, 1974.

4. Coastal Zone Management: Multiple Use with Conservation;
    Brahtz; J. Wiley, New York, 1972.

5. Tourism and Development; Bryden; Cambridge UP; 1973.

6. Conservation in Practice; Warren and Goldsmith; J. Wiley,
    New York, 1974.

7. Elements of Tourism Policy in Developing Countries; UN (UNCTAI
    Geneva/New York, 1973.

8. Tourism and Environment: The Search for a Balance; Haulot
    Marabout, Verviers, 1974.

9. The Environmental Revolution; Nicholson, Penguin, London, 1972.

10. Tourism, Blessing or Blight? Young; Penguin, London.

11. Outdoor Recreation for America; ORRRC; Washington, USA, 1962.

12. National Parks for the Future; Conservation Foundation, USA,
    1972.

13. Design with Nature; McHarg; Natural History Press, USA, 1971.

14. Ecological Principles for Economic Development; Dasmann;
    J. Wiley, 1973.

15. Economics of Outdoor Recreation; Clawson and Knetch; Hopkins
    Press, Baltimore, 1966.

16. Natural Environment: Studies in Theoretical and Applied Analyses;
    Krutilla, Hopkins Press, Baltimore, 1972.

17. Social Behaviour, Natural Resources and the Environment; Burch,
    Cheek and Taylor; Harper and Row, London, 1972.

18. Planning for Tourism Development - Quantitative Approaches,
     Gearing; Praeger.

19. Land and Leisure - Concept and Methods in Outdoor Recreation;
     Fischer, Lewis and Priddle; Maarafa Press, Chicago, 1974.

20. Three Reports on Conservation of the Environment and Tourism -
     Development; Travis: CURS/STB/OECD respectively 1977;
     1974; 1978.

BIBLIOGRAPHY ON ENVIRONMENT
AND TOURISM

The following bibliography provides a selection of publications dealing with tourism and related environmental consideration. It covers only a certain number of OECD Member countries participating in the project and the publications listed are limited mainly to those provided by the participating countries.

ENVIRONMENTAL POLICIES
(MEANS AND MEASURES)

"Planning and Development of Recreational Areas, including the Development of the Natural Environment"

> United Nations, New York, 1969.
> Economic Commission for Europe.
> 2 volumes, 386 p. , annexes (Engl. Fr.).
>
> Basic components of recreation policy: environmental, economic, social and policy aims.
> Planning of recreational areas (criteria, standards, aids).
> Country-by-country examples of:
> - policies for promoting recreation and development of the natural environment;
> - planning recreational areas;
> - creating recreational areas.

"Elements of Macro-Planning in Tourism Development"

> Prof. Dr. Salah-Eldln Abdel Wahab
> AIEST (International Association of Scientific Experts in Tourism).
> The Tourist Review, No. 2, April/June 1973, 10 p. (Engl.).
>
> Proposed guidelines for a tourism development plan.
> Tourism physical planning as a part of the overall tourism development plan. Planning process, components and levels.
> Individualisation, classification and assessment of tourism resources within the planning context.

"The Protection of Coastal Areas"

J. A. Steers
Council of Europe, 1974, 87 p. (Engl. , Fr.).
The European Information Centre for Nature Conservation.

Basic principles for a policy to safeguard coastal areas
associated with some degree of tourism development. Protection
of coastal areas in various European countries (Spain, France,
Italy, Cyprus, Turkey, Malta, the Netherlands, Federal Republic
of Germany, Sweden, Norway, Belgium, Ireland and the United
Kingdom).

"Legislative Measures taken or to be taken by the Member States
of the Council of Europe for the Protection of the Coastline".

Prof. Amselek, Jonathan Cohen, Prof. Prieur.
Council of Europe. 1974. 149 p. (Engl. Fr.).
The European Information Centre for Nature Conservation.

General protective instruments at national and international levels.
Protection policies (in particular with regard to the use of the
coastline for tourism).
Conservation of natural and historical resources.   Pollution
control.

"Planning and Development of the Tourist Industry in the ECE Region"

Economic Commission for Europe.
Proceedings of the Symposium on the Planning and Development
of the Tourist Industry in the ECE Region held under the auspices
of ECE at Dubrovnik (Yugoslavia), 13-18 October 1975.
United Nations.   New York 1976.   198 pages. (Fr. Engl.).

Discussion on specific topics relating to tourist industry development:
- physical planning
- social implications
- environmental implications:
    formulation of norms for carrying capacity, the cultural
    heritage as a basic asset of tourist industry development,
    control of pollution arising from tourism or obstructing its
    further development
- economic implications:
    measurement and evaluation of costs and benefits, impact of
    tourism on employment, future demand of tourism and its factors
- methodology for integrated socio-economic environmental
    planning
- overall strategies and policy measures
- recommendations.

"Tourism Policy and International Tourism in OECD Member Countries"

> Organisation for Economic Co-operation and Development, Paris, 1978 (published annually), 195 p. (Fr. , Engl.).
>
> Government policy and action concerned with tourism (especially as regards the environment, regional planning and employment). International tourist flows in Member countries. The importance of tourism in international payments. Transport, tourist accommodation, statistics.

"Impact of Tourism on the Environment and Existing or Needed Associated Environmental Measures"
"Tourism and Environment"

> AIEST (International Association of Scientific Experts in Tourism). Reports presented to the 21st Congress of the AIEST, 5-13 September 1971, Puerto de la Cruz (Tenerife), Vol. 11, 94 p.
>
> Editions Gurten, Gurtenverlag, Berne, Switzerland (Ger. , Engl. , Sp. , Fr.).
>
> Tourism and the environmental problems induced by its growth (physiological, psychological, technical, architectural, legal and economic aspects).
> Policies and measures to protect the environment in various countries.

"Congrès d'écologie et tourisme de la Méditerranée Occidentale. Textes et Documents". Madrid. 30 octobre-3 novembre 1972. 441 p. (Sp. , Fr.).

> Analysis of the impact of tourism on the natural environment (continental and coastal) and upon the urban environment of the mediterranean regions: causes of deterioration and consequences. Actions and measures required to protect the environment, in policy and legislation.

"Recreational Needs as Factors of Regional and Agricultural Development"

> Internal information on agriculture.
> Commission of the European Communities.
> Directorate-General VI Agriculture, Brussels.
> No. 116, November 1973, 107 p. (annexes), (Engl. , Fr.).
>
> General data regarding tourism. Possible tourism planning policy guidelines for promoting regional development.
> Effects of tourism on the regional economy and the rural environment.

Estimates of tourism demand up to 1980 (land, investment and employment requirements) for planning purposes in EEC Member States.
Outline of a planning and budgetary control system in tourism and recreation.

"Les dévoreurs de paysages : le tourisme doit-il détruire les sites qui le font vivre ?"

Jost Krippendorf. Editions 24 heures, Lausanne, 1977, 157 p. , (Fr. Ger.).

Disintegration and deterioration of recreational areas as a result of tourism. Suggested landscape conservation measures.

"L'habitat des loisirs et la résidence seconde dans l'aménagement du territoire"

Journées Aménagement et Nature, 30-31 octobre 1968. Documents préparatoires et comptes-rendus, No. 13, March 1969, 85 p. ; No. 15, September 1969, 28 p. (Fr.).

Problems raised by the various forms of recreation in several European countries (deterioration of sites, types of natural environment, etc.). Socio-economic effects upon the rural environment. Definition of a policy enabling recreational areas to be smoothly incorporated in land-use planning.

"European Technical Conference on Recreation and Nature Conservancy", Hamburg, 9th-13th June, 1975.

- Topic 1: "Planning of recreational areas and nature conservancy in densely populated regions"

Dr. Walter Mrass (Germany), 25 p.

The different types of recreational area in conurbations. Planning problems in areas deserving protection.

- Topic 2: "Planning of recreational areas and nature conservancy in coastal, lake and river regions"

G. Tendron (France), 38 p.

The various forms of recreation and effects on the aquatic and surrounding environment. Planning of recreational areas and protection of the environment.

- Topic 3: "Planning of recreational areas and nature conservancy in mountain regions"

Dr. Theo Hunziker and Dr. Willi Zeller (Switzerland), 35 p.

Objectives of recreation planning and adequate recommended measures in the European context.
General principles of nature conservancy in recreation planning.
Effects of various forms of recreation on mountain regions.
Examples of Swiss resorts incorporating environmental protection in the planning process.

"Tourism and the Environment"

Mohamed Tangi.
Ambio. A journal of the human environment, research and management. The Mediterranean. A special issue. Volume VI, No. 6, 1977, p. 336-341. Royal Swedish Academy of Sciences, Universitetsforlaget (Engl.).

Analysis of tourism in the Mediterranean region.
Impact of tourism on natural, man-made and socio-cultural environment.
Alternative development patterns for the tourist industry.

"Endangered Alpine Regions and Disaster Prevention Measures"

Prof. Dr. H. Aulitzky
Council of Europe, Strasbourg, France, 1974.
No. 6, Nature and Environment Series, 106 p. (Engl., Fr.).

Reasons for the growing number of natural disasters in the alpine regions:
- changes in the structure of the population, human activities and land use, largely due to tourism;
- specific natural conditions "in balance".
Prevention measures in the Alpine States and the efforts to achieve international co-operation.

"Strategies for Tourism Development in Mountain Regions"

Final report by G. Feurstein (Austria).
Council of Europe, Committee on Co-operation in Municipal and Regional Matters, 1976, 38 p. (Ger., Engl., Fr.).

Formulation of basic principles for a common European tourism policy in mountain regions with the help of ten case studies which analyse:
- the status of tourism development and the role of the local population;
- problems and conflicts due to tourism development (capacity, facilities, jobs, problems of land-use, nature conservancy and environmental protection).

"The Impact of Tourism upon Regional Economies"

B. H. Archer.
Local Government Finance, No. 6, 1971, p. 183-185 (Engl.).

Effects of tourist spending on regional employment, incomes ...
The multiplier effect.

"The Role of Tourism in Economic Development. Is it a benefit or a
burden ?"

International Tourism Quarterly.
The Economist Intelligence Unit, No. 2, 1973, p. 53-68 (Engl.).

Adverse and beneficial economic effects of the growth of international tourism, especially in developing countries.

"The Impacts of Tourism and Recreational Facility Development"

Jack L. Knetsch and Turgut Var.
AIEST (International Association of Scientific Experts in Tourism).

The Tourist Review. No. 4, 1976, p. 5-9 (Engl.).

Economic, environmental and social impacts of tourism.

"Tourism and Coastal Environment"

Arthur Haulot.
AIEST (International Association of Scientific Experts in Tourism).

The Tourist Review. No. 1, January/March 1978, p. 10-12 (Engl.).

Recreational role of beaches and coastal areas. Reasons for
increasing demand for coastal space and implications for environment. Need for planning.

"L'aménagement physique du territoire"

in "L'aménagement touristique du territoire", New Delhi Seminar,
IUOTO, Geneva, March 1973, 26 pages.

Describes the various forms of interaction between the natural or
man-made environment and tourism, which in fact encourage
tourism; warns that tourism could well constitute the greatest
threat to the world's most celebrated tourist attractions; points
out the interdependence of tourism with other sectors of a
country's economy; identifies a number of basic land-use planning
principles applicable to tourism development.

IMPACT OF TOURISM ON THE ENVIRONMENT

AUSTRALIA

"The Impact of Tourism on the Environment"

Walter, R. D.

Melbourne, Australian Recreation Research Association, 1975,
190 p.
Available: Arch. Library, Melbourne University.

A report on the general characteristics of tourism, the demand
for tourism, the supply of tourist resources and numbers of
tourists. The impacts of tourism on the economic, social,
political and physical elements of the environment are examined.
The compatibility of tourism and conservation is questioned and
doubts are raised as to whether the concept of carrying capacity
has any utility in the planning of tourist regions and facilities.

"Conservation and Wilderness Recreation". Research commenced
in 1960 for the Australian Conservation Foundation

Mosley, J. G.

A study of visitors' understanding and appreciation of wilderness
areas, based on area surveys, user interviews and questionnaires,
and study of departmental files, reports, activities, etc.

"The Environmental Impact of Outdoor Recreation". In Victoria's
Resources, September/November, 1972, p. 11-16

Mercer, D.

Lists areas where tourism is affecting the landscape and gives
details of type of land activity practiced and the results of the
time effected.

"The Impact of Possible Tourist Development on the Upper Ovens Valley"

Melbourne, Environment Studies Association of Victoria, 1975,
35 p. , $2.40.

This report considers the problems of future tourist and recreation
development in relation to a small mountain township, Harrietville,
and on wilderness and recreation areas on Mt. Feathertop and
Mt. Hotham, where the local 'social economy', landforms and

landscapes may each be seen as placing serious constraints on the type, amount and siting of further facilities for tourists and recreationers.

Victoria. Environment Studies Association.

"The Impact of the Ski Village on the Alpine Environment of the Baw Baw Plateau"

Melbourne, Environment Studies Association of Victoria, 1973, 9 p., $1.10.

This report considers the present and potential recreational uses of the Baw Baw Plateau, the impact of the ski village and a study of the village as a functional unit.

"Tourism and its Environmental Impacts in Arid Australia". Est. completion 1980.

Mabbut, J. A. (University of NSW).

Part of a wider study of the problems of arid lands development and the environmental impacts of such developments. Initiated for the UN Conference on Desertification (1977) and continuing.

"Community Research in Environmental and Regional Planning" p. 1-23 of Papers Presented at the North Coast Research Review

Douglas, I.

Newcastle, Board of Environmental Studies and Department of Community Programs, University of Newcastle, 1977.

A research review by University of New England staff of the development of the North Coast of New South Wales with emphasis on land-use conflicts associated with tourism.

Extensive bibliography.

ENVIRONMENTAL POLICIES
(MEANS AND MEASURES)

"Hunter 2000 - Conservation of Lands and Buildings of Natural, Historical, Scenic or Recreational Value in the Hunter Region"

National Trust of Australia (New South Wales).
Newcastle, 1972, 44 p., $1.70.

Prepared at the request of the State Planning Authority of New South Wales to assist in the development of planning proposals in the Hunter Region. Based on field research in the Hunter District during 1971 and 1972.

"Sydney 2000 - Requirements for Conservation of Natural Areas, Scenic Preservation and Recreation"

Setchell, G. H.

Sydney, 1968, 44 p. , $1.40.

"Policies of the Australian Conservation Foundation"

Australian Conservation Foundation.
Melbourne, 1971, 38 p.

Statement of the ACF Policies: Preservation and Conservation of animal and plant species; areas of special national significance; nature conservation; land-use and resource planning.

"Management of Conservation Reserves"

Australian Conservation Foundation.
Melbourne, 1972.

Outlines the need for landscape management, the classification of reserves, objectives of recreation reserves and wildlife conservation.

"Conservation Study of Stanley"

Hobart.
Bush, Parkes, Shugg and Moon, 1975, 92 p.

Available: Department of Tourism, Hobart.

A conservation study of Stanley township and seaport, commissioned by Circular Head Municipal Council. Contains an inventory of historic and natural features on the area and recommends policies for the preservation of these features.

"Conservation of the Australian Coast"

Australian Conservation Foundation.
Melbourne, 1972, 77 p. (Special Publication No. 7), $1.50.

Papers from a symposium on the Australian Coast.
Symposium divided into four sections: Perspectives; Industries and Effluents; The Living Coast; People, Planning and Pleasure.

"Coast Management - Qld - NSW Border to Northern Boundary of Noosa Shire - Volume 1". The Report.

> Gutteridge, Haskins and Davey (Consultants).
> 1975, 151 p.
>
> Available: Queensland Co-ordinator-General's Dept.
>
> See particularly Section 8 "Proposals for Recreation and Conservation".

IMPACT OF TOURISM ON THE ENVIRONMENT AND EXISTING OR NEEDED ASSOCIATED ENVIRONMENTAL MEASURES

"Environmental Characterization Report",
Ayers Rock - Mt. Olga National Park.

> Arid Zone Research Institute.
> Alice Springs, AGPS, 1972, 100 pages, maps, tables.
>
> A description of the geology, geomorphology, climate, surface hydrology, soils, vegetation and fauna of the Ayers Rock - Mt. Olga National Park. Separate section describes land units- soils, vegetation and recorded fauna. An environmental effects of an expanded tourist industry section offers prescription for ecological protection.

"A Study of the Impact of Tourism at Ayers Rock - Mt. Olga National Park"

> J. D. Ovington, K. W. Growes, P. R. Stevens and M. T. Tanton.
>
> Australia. Department of Interior.
> Canberra, 1972, 142 pages.
>
> The impact of tourism around and on Ayers Rock is documented, and a new technique to determine the carrying capacity of the Park for tourists applied. Detailed recommendations are made of management techniques to meet the needs of tourists without further environmental deterioration. Based on original research in the area during 1972. Observation of tourist activities, measurement of vegetation, soil and topography change. Determination of carrying capacity by summation method.

"Conservation and Tourism in Central Australia: Ecological conservation project".

Australian Tourist Commission.
Melbourne, 1972, 80 p.

Outlines the area under consideration in terms of physical and biologic environment. Gives the needs for conservation and the actions necessary by the tourist industry. Lists future trends and conflicts with possible solutions and also recommendations.

"Metropolitan Coast Protection District Study Report"

Pak-Poy (PG) and Associates Pty Ltd.

Adelaide, 1974, 150 p.

A report prepared for SA Coast Protection Board. The aims were to:

1. Collect date on the Metropolitan Coast Protection District which has relevance to the current and future use of the district.

2. Determine policies for management, and the type and location of coastal facilities, to accommodate the activities of metropolitan residents and visitors.

Proposals include upgrading and integration of foreshore reserves with the beaches; provision of off-street parking; beach replenishment program; establishment of a coastal plant nursery.

"Augusta: Tourism and Recreation" - Report on Tourism and Recreation for the Environmental Study of the Blackwood River Estuary Project, Technical Report 12.

Perth, Department of Conservation and Environment, 1976.
Available: Department of Conservation and Environment.

"A Coastal Retreat"

Melbourne, Victorian Public Interest Group 1977, 270 p.

A study of the causes and extent of the down grading of the quality of the coast as a scenic conservation and recreation area. Two study areas were selected, one from Torquay to Peterborough, the other from Cape Paterson to Shallow Inlet. The report looks into their natural and cultural histories, recreation potentials and demands, the attitudes of coast users, coastal land use, the management bodies involved in controlling coastal land use, and the extent and effectiveness of town and country planning.

"The Future of the Great Barrier Reef"

Australian Conservation Foundation.
Melbourne, 1969. 69 p. (Special Publication No. 3). $1.50.

Papers of an ACF symposium on the Great Barrier Reef. Topics included marine biology; limestone mining; legal aspects of the Great Barrier Reef; fisheries, off-shore petroleum exploration and production; and tourism and recreation.

"Conservation of Cockburn Sound, Western Australia; A Case Study"

R. G. Chittleborough.
Melbourne, 1970. 27 p. (Special Publication No. 5). $0.50

Report on Cockburn Sound and the requirements for conservation of its resources, which the ACF regards of national significance.

AUSTRIA

"Beiträge zur Abklärung von Grundsatsfragen der Belastung und der Belastbarkeit im Alpenraum. Generelle Problemanalyse, Ubersicht über Lösungsansätze, Empfehlungen"

(D. Bernt, G. Ruhl u. a.)

Alpeninstitut für Umweltforschung und Entwicklungsplanung und Osterreichisches Institut für Raumplanung

(Seminar über Probleme der Belastung und der Raumplanung im Berggebiet, insbesondere in den Alpen, Grindelwald (Schweiz) vom. 13.-16. Juni 1978)

"Belastbarkeitsgrenzen im Hinblick auf den Fremdenverkehr in der Region Kitzbühel"

Amt der Tiroler Landesregierung, Abteilung I c - Landesplanung

(Insbruck 1978)

"Untersuchung Raumbezogener Probleme der Fremdenverkehrsentwicklung in Montafon"

Amt der Vorarlberger Landesregierung (Raumplanungsstelle) und Osterreichisches Institut für Raumplanung (OIR)

(D. Bernt, V. Fleischhacker, P. Haimayer, H. Tiefenthaler)

"Die Bedeutung der Landschaftsökologie für die Erholungslandschaft"

Bierhals, E.

In: Wasser für die Erholungslandschaft; Hrsq.: Bayerische
Biologische Versuchsanstalt, München 1975 (= Münchener
Beiträge zur Abwasser-, Fischerei- und Flussbiologie, Bd. 26),
S. 13-26.

"Das Modell Obergurgl. Ein Mikrokosmos: Wirtschaftswachstum
im Begrenzten Raum"

Bunnell, F. , Bunnell, P. , Buckingham, S. , Hilborn, R. ,
Margreiter, G. , Moser, W. , Walters, C.

(Internationales Institut für Angewandie Systemanalyse,
Laxenburg, Osterreich)

Alpine Areas Workshop, 13. -17. 5. 1974.

"Alpine Umweltprobleme. I. Okologische Veränderungen durch das
Anlegen von Schiabfahrten an Waldhängen"

CERNUSCA, A. (Hrsg.)

Berlin 1977.

"Die Belastbarkeit des Landes Salzburg mit Zweitwohnungen"

Cziharz, G. , Kyrer, A. , Pichler, W. u. a.

(Erster Teil). Salzburg 1973.

"Landschaftsbewertung für Erholungszwecke. Modelluntersuchung
Virgental, Osttirol"

Engelhardt, W. , Weinzierl, W.

Wien 1976.

"Tourismus und Umwelt in Osterreich"

Gepp, J. , Plank, St. , Zimmerman, A.

(Ludwig Boltzmann-Institut für Umweltwissenschaften und
Naturschutz, Graz)

Wien 1978.

"Zur Frage der Ganzjahresschigebiete: Das Beispiel Hochstubai/
Tirol"

Haimayer, P.

Aus: Berichte zur Raumforschung und Raumplanung, 21 (1977),
1, 12 S.

"Die Belastbarkeit des Landes Salzburg mit Zweitwohnungen"
(Zweiter Teil)

Hutter, H.

Salzburg 1978.

"Dokumentation von Lösungsmöglichkeiten"

Infraconsult AG, Bern, (Federführung: U. Roth) in Zusammenar-
beit mit Urbaplan, Lausanne, Osterreichischem Institut für
Raumplanung, Wien, Alpeninstitut für Umweltforschung und
Entwicklungsplanung, München, Metron, Brugg, unter Mithilfe
des Secrétariat du Comité des Hauts Fonctionnaires, Division de
l'Aménagement du Territoire, des Monuments et Sites du Conseil
de l'Europe.

Seminarbericht, Teil III (Europäische Raumordnungsministerkonfe
enz, komittee der Hohen Beamten - Seminar über Probleme der
Belastung und der Raumplanung im Berggebiet, insbesondere in
den Alpen, Grindelwalt (Schweiz) vom 13.-16. Juni 1978).

"Mab-6 Obergurgl"

Moser, W.

In: Mensch und Biosphäre Projekt Nr. 6, ICC-Vienna, 24. Okt. -
1 Nov. 1977, Wien 1977, S. 74-97.

"Vorlagebericht für den Arbeitsausschuss "Umwelt" zum
Osterreichischen Fremdenverkahrstag 1976"

Osterreichischer Gemeindebund

Wien 1976.

"Ratschläge zur Vermeidung und Bereinigung von Oberlastungen der
Touristischen Landschaft"

Osterreichischer Gemeindebund

Entwurf, Wien 1976.

"Fremdenverkehrs-planung Neusiedlersee"

Osterreichisches Institut für Raumplanung (Bearb.: D. Bernt, H. Palme)

Wien 1970.

"Die Raumansprüche von Writschaft, Siedlung, Verkehr, Naturschutz, Bundesheer"

Osterreichisches Institut für Raumplanung (Bearb.: D. Bernt)

Wien 1970.

"Vorschläge zum Entwicklungs-programm Neusiedlersee"

Osterreichisches Institut für Raumplanung (Bearb.: D. Bernt)

Wien 1970.

"Alpine Berggebiete - Städtische Agglomerationen"

Osterreichisches Institut für Raumplanung (Bearb.: V. Fleischhacker, D. Bernt u. a.): Studie über die wichtigsten Verflechtungen des österreichischen Alpenraumes mit Agglomerationen

Wien 1975.

"Grundlagen fur das Seminar über Probleme der Belastung und der Raumplanung im Berggebiet": insbesondere in den Alpen, Gridelwald (Schweiz) vom 13. bis 16. Juni 1978, Haupstudie I

Osterreichisches Institut für Raumplanung

(Bearb.: D. Bernt, A. Cerny)

Wien 1978.

"Entwicklungsplan Pongau - Teilkonzept Landschaft/Arbeit-smethode zur Berechnung der touristischen Kapazitat und Belastbarkeit - Beispiel Grossarltal"

Planpartner Paula Wien

Im Auftrag des Amtes der Salzburger Landesregierung, Abt. VII, UAbt. Landesplanung und Raumordnung

Wien 1977 (unveröffentlight).

"Der Piburger See (Otztal, Tirol) als Freizeitraum"

Haimayer, P.

Ein Beitrag zur Frage der Belastbarkeit touristischer
Landschaften. In: Innsbrucker Geographische Studien, Bd. 6.

"Zweitwohnungen für Freizeit und Erholung"

Institut für Geographie der Universität Innsbruch
(P. Haimayer).

"Okologisches Gutachten zum Wasserwirtschaftlichen Rahmenplan
für das Iselgebiet, Osttirol. Fachgutachten: Die zu erwartenden
Veranderungen des Landschaftsbildes und ihre Auswirkungen"

Kastner, F.

2 Bde.

Wien 1978.

CANADA

"Impact économique du Tourisme dans les Chic-Chocs (Gaspésie)"

Robert Avossa
Ministère du Tourisme, de la Chasse et de la Pêche,
Service de la Recherche, Québec, mars 1973, 131 p. (Fr.).

The economic impact of tourism in the Chic-Chocs and the
criteria for developing recreational sources of the region with
the aim of providing facilities for tourists which will also make
a contribution to the local economy.

"Retombées socio-économiques d'un développement touristique:
théorie et application"

Faouzi F. Rassi
Ministère du Tourisme, de la Chasse et de la Pêche,
Série méthodologique, Volume IV, 1975, 557 p.

A general methodology to be used in tourism research, forecasting, cost-benefit analysis

Estimation of tourist flows and investment requirements between
1972 and 1982. Training and retraining of the required work-force.

114

"Some Social Costs and Benefits of Tourism to Rural Communities. The Cape Cod Case"

Abraham Pizam, Ernest J. Acquaro
Department of Hotel, Restaurant and Travel Administration
Research Bulletin No. 649, 1977, 84 p. (Engl.)
Published by the Massachussets Agricultural Experiment Station.

Social, Economic and Demographic Characteristics of Tourists, Residents and Entrepreneurs of Tourism in Cape Cod. Attitudes of Residents and Entrepreneurs towards Tourists and Impacts of Tourism.

"Inventaire des Terres du Canada. Potentiel des Terres à des Fins Récréatives"

Brown C. S. /Hargrave M. M. /Gavin H. C. R. et divers.
Ministère de l'Expansion Economique Régionale, Ottawa,
Rapport No. 6, 97 pages, cartes, photos.

The objective of this land-use classification for recreational purposes is to provide global of the quality, the degree of utilization and siting of areas suitable for recreation and to establish the various degrees of recreational policy of non-urban areas, to determine the type of recreation for which the areas are most suitable, and to identify the areas where the characteristics are of exceptional or unique recreational value.

FRANCE

"Tourisme et milieu rural. Zone Vendée"

Institut National de Gestion et d'Economie Rurale (IGER).
CREDAR, Ministère de l'Agriculture,
        Direction Générale de l'Espace Rural, 1969, 175 p. ,
annexe (Fr.)

Siting conditions, patterns and types of seaside tourism development in nine rural communes on the Vendée coast. Impact of tourism on the environment (agriculture, commerce; crafts).

"Mesure des effets socio-économiques du tourisme sur le littoral aquitain"

CRESI, Commissariat Général au Tourisme, 1973, 62 p. (Fr.).

Methods of analysing the tourism process and its effects (incomes, employment) on the Aquitaine coast.
The socio-economic impact of tourism in various types of resort area (countryside, coast, mountain).

"Incidences économiques de l'aménagement touristique de la Côte Aquitaine"

J. Mesplier et E. Le mainque
Knstitut d'Economie Régionale du Sud-Ouest (IERSO),
OREAM Bordeaux-Aquitaine, 1974, 2 volumes (53 p. and 86 p.),
(Fr.)

An attempt to measure the effects of the turnover from the tourism industry upon the regional economy. How the tertiary sector adapts to seasonal tourist movements along the Aquitaine Coast.

"L'aménagement de la zone littorale Pas-de-Calais et Mer du Nord. Présentation dynamique du littoral, conflits d'utilisation de l'espace et prospective. Thèmes possibles de réflexion"

International Seminar, 26th-27th January, 1978, Dunkerque-Boulogne.
Introductory Report, BETURE, 62 p. (Fr.).

Discusses the use made of land for tourism and recreation along the Pas-de-Calais and North Sea coasts of France; characteristics and effects: urbanization, saturation processes, financial difficulties, conflicts with traditional economic activities, destruction of the natural environment. Forecasting of factors promoting change, in coastal areas and their consequences.

"Relations Tourisme-Aquaculture"

Rapport du CEASM (CNEXO), August 1974, 127 p. (Fr.)

Conflicts arising out of the development of two economic activities with diverging interests: tourism and fish-farming. Analyses of the effects of intensified tourism on production structures and land use.

116

"L'aménagement de la côte entre Mention et Théoule (Alpes-Maritimes et Monaco). Inventaire des restructurations du rivage et impacts sur la vie sous-marine littorale"

A. Meinesz et J. R. Lefèvre
SOS Vie, Nature, Environnement. N° spécial 19, 1976, 35 p.
(Fr.)

Lists alterations to the coastline between Mention and Théoule to meet tourism requirements (marinas, enclosed beaches, reclaimed land) and their impact on underwater animal and plant life.

"Impact économique et conditions de financement des ports de plaisance"

SEATL, Secrétariat d'Etat au Tourisme.
DPMVN, Ministère de l'Equipement et de l'Aménagement du Territoire,
1976, 32 p. , (Fr.)

Construction costs, financing and operating procedures for marinas.
Economic impact of marinas (employment, expenditures by users, commercial, real-estate implications).

"Au tribunal des ruraux"

Espaces-Tourisme, Loisirs, Environnement.
N° 2, janvier 1974, p. 38-40 (Fr.)

Findings of a survey conducted among residents of the Central and West Atlantic coastal area: attitudes towards tourism as a cause of change.

"Cinq résidences secondaires nouvelles à l'heure"

Marc Thomas
Espace, N° 71, mai 1977, p. 3-14 (Fr.)

Growth of secondary homes by region.
Impact upon the countryside, community infrastructure, the real-estate market and the environment.

"L'impact du développement des résidences secondaires dans les communes rurales"

M. Perchet et G. Codet
Atelier Régional d'Etudes Economiques et d'Aménagement Rural de Franche-Comté. Besançon, SIER, 1974, 48 p. , annexes (Fr.)

General characteristics marking the growth of secondary homes. Economic and social repercussions and implications for local government.

"Résidences secondaires et aménagement du cadre de vie"

Meryem le Saget
Mémoire HECJF, Paris, 1973, 198 p. (Fr.)

Quantitative and qualitative analysis of the growth of secondary homes; how they fit into the tourism process; economic and social consequences; development within France's urban context.

"Les résidences secondaires en France dans le cadre de l'habitat de loisir"

by the Group: "Aménagement et Nature",
Paris, Documentation Française, NED N° 3939-3940, 1972, 88 p. (Fr.)

Analyses the secondary-home process (measurement, trends, siting). Effects on local economy (agriculture, commerce, crafts, employment, local finances), on the land-use patterns, local architecture, and on the human and natural habitats.

"Résidences secondaires, tourisme rural et enjeux locaux. Habitat de loisir, économie locale et gestion municipale dans quatre communes rurales de la région Provence-Côte d'Azur"

C. Dourlens et P. Vidal Naquet
DRE Provence-Alpes-Côte d'Azur,
Centre d'Etudes du Tourisme, Aix-en-Provence, 1978, 257 p. (Fr.)

Effects of secondary homes on the local economy (land prices, marketing of agricultural products, employment, local finances).

"Tourisme et milieu rural"

Institut National de Gestion et d'Economie Rurale (IGER).
Ministère de l'Agriculture, 1969, 107 p. (Fr.)

Types of accommodation and of clientele in the countryside.
Tourist expenditure and activities.
Economic and social effects on the countryside (resources, activities, incomes).

"Le tourisme, facteur de transformation du milieu rural ?"

Institut National de Gestion et d'Economie Rurale (IGER).
Espaces, Tourisme, Loisirs, Environnement.
No. 3, January-March 1971, p. 55-56 (Fr.)

Economic, social and land-holding changes brought about by
tourism.
The various changes due to tourism, as illustrated in four
geographical areas (break-up of traditional patterns, juxtaposition
of two economies, redeployment of those previously in traditional
occupations).

"La fonction touristique de l'espace rural. Bilan et perspectives
d'avenir"

SEGESA (Société d'Etudes Géographiques Economiques et Socio-
logiques Appliquées)
Commissariat Général du Plan, 1971, 62 p. (Fr.)

Characteristics of rural tourism. Effects on employment,
economic activity, demography, attitudes, the living environment
and local finances.

"Situation économique et financière d'une commune résidentielle et
touristique : Sausset-les-Pins"

C. Dourlens et P. Vidal Naquet
DRE Provence-Alpes-Côte d'Azur,
Centre d'Etudes du Tourisme, Aix-en-Provence, 1978, 42 p. ,
(Fr.), annexes.

Impact of tourism on local finances.

"Impact des stations touristiques sur la société locale. Les Alpes
du Sud"

CTGREF Service régional de l'Equipement Provence-Côte d'Azur,
Grenoble.
Ministères de l'Equipement et de l'Agriculture.
1976, 2 volumes (333 p. and 304 p.), (Fr.)

Shows how local communities in the Southern Alpes have evolved
in response to various types of tourism development. Analyses
seven resorts, from when they were first established, through
their impact on economic patterns, local finances, jobs, agriculture and socio-demographic trends.

"L'implantation d'une station de sports d'hiver et ses répercussions sur le monde rural. Un exemple parmi d'autres : Saint-Martin-de-Belleville"

J. Guéret
Options Méditerranéennes, No. 3, septembre/octobre 1970, p. 108-110 (Fr.)

Development of a winter sports resort and consequences for land-use planning, farming and employment.

"Problèmes économiques liés à l'assainissement du lac d'Annecy"

J. P. Deportes
Mémoire de l'Institut National de la Recherche Agronomique et de l'Ecole Nationale Supérieure Agronomique de Rennes 1972, 62 p. , (Fr.)

Studies the effects of eutrophication and cleansing of Lake Annecy on various sectors of the economy, especially tourism trends, which is analysed by means of such significant indicators as expenditures by tourists, hotel turnover, nights spent, accommodation, etc.

"Le rôle du tourisme dans la croissance économique"

G. Cazes
AIEST (International Association of Scientific Experts in Tourism)
The Tourist Review, No. 3 July/September 1972,
                        No. 4 October/December 1972, 11 p. (Fr.)

The economic impact of tourism in three developing West-Indian islands, Puerto-Rico, Antigua and Jamaica.

"Aspects économiques du tourisme"

R. Baretje et P. Defert
Collection "l'administration nouvelle"
Editions Berger-Levrault. Paris, 1972, 355 p. (Fr.)

Part I, Chapters 5 and 6, pp. 97-127, Title II,
"L'espace touristique", deals with the real-estate problems of tourism in town and country planning.
Part II, Chapter 12, Title II,
"Des effets de la dépense touristique" discusses the effects of tourism expenditure and tourism as an inflationary factor.

"Aspects du tourisme"

Economie et Humanisme, No. 226, November/December 1975,
p. 2-63 (Fr.)

"Les vacances : concentration ou étalement ?", by F. Camuset,
discusses the socio-economic consequences of concentrating
holidays
"Le temps partagé : solution d'avenir aux problèmes des
résidences de loisirs ?" by G. Guibilato, discusses the impact
of secondary homes upon the areas concerned.
"Réflexions sur l'aménagement touristique du Languedoc-
Roussillon" by R. Baretje and J. M. Thurot discusses the socio-
economic effects of tourism development in Languedoc-Roussillon
upon various sectors (employment, agriculture and industry).

"Introduction de données et objectifs environnementaux dans la planification régionale. Loisirs/Tourisme et Environnement"

Ministère de la Culture et de l'Environnement
Service des Affaires Générales, 1977, 42 p. (Fr.)

Recreation and its environmental effects (on the natural environment, overloading and the concept of capacity).
The Alsace region as a case study.
Recreation "policy" in Alsace. Methods of evaluating various
aspects of the relationships between recreation and the environment and trends.
Annexes: Suggested system for classifying effects of tourism upon
the environment.

ITALY

"Turismo e svilupo economico"

Alberto Bertolino
Economia del Turismo, Italia, Etas Kompass, Milano, 1969,
p. 1-2 (Ital.)

Analyses the main features of the tourism process in technical
terms: supply and demand, induced effects, socio-economic
consequences, internal and external, in the context of economic
development.
The need for a tourism policy.

"Le rôle des initiatives humaines locales dans un développement touristique : la réussite exceptionnelle de Riccione (Région de Rimini)"

L. Coulet
Les Cahiers du Tourisme, Série B N° 10,
Centre d'Etudes du Tourisme, Aix-en-Provence, 1969, 46 pages
(Fr.)

The major international seaside resort of Riccione as a case study. Factors in the change from an agricultural to a tourist economy: land speculation, use of real estate, a short-term credit system. Problems caused by tourism development.

NETHERLANDS

"Natuur en recreatie in St. Jansberg en Mookerheide; een vergelijkende studie t. b. v. het beheer van een natuurgebied, waar veelvuldig recreatie gebruik van wordt gemaakt"

Dankelman, Irene

Wageningen, L. H. Natuurbeheer, 1977, 147 p.

"Kamperen op natuurkampeerterrein; een onderzoek onder kampeerder op een zestal natuurkampeerterreinen van het Staatsbosbeheer"

Biermans, H. W. M.

Utrecht, Staatsbosbeheer, 1976. III. Bos en rekreatie;
8. Rapport Staatsbosbeheer. 1976, 159 p.

"Onderzoek naar de invloed van de recreatiedichtheid op de begroeiing van natuurterreinen in het Gooi en zijn randgebieden"

A. M. Bakker, H. M. Haarsma, M. Laurentius

Rivon rapport, 1975, 48 p.

"Bezoekerstellingen in CRM natuurreservaten"

Peltzer, R. H. M.

Rapport Staatsbosbeheer afd. Recreatie-onderzoek, 1976,
145 p.

"De Biesbosch ... vaarwell! ? onderzoek naar de mogelijkheden van recreatie en waterwinning in een kwetsbaar natuurgebied. Deel A, hoofd-rapport"

I. S. P. Biesbosch TH Delft. Rapportnr. 1039A, 1976, 104 p.

"De invloed van de recreatie op de broedvogels van bos en duin op het eiland Vlieland"

Koersveld, S. van and A. Kooij

Wageningen, L. H. - Natuurbehoud en beheer, 1976, $\pm$ 70 p.

"Openluchtrecreatie en nationale landschapsparken; studie naar functie en betekenis van openluchtreacreatie in nationale landschapsparken gemaakt in opdracht van het ministerie van CRM"

Maas, Buro

Staatsuitgeverij, 's-Gravenhage, 1977, 183 p.

"Onderzoek naar de invloed van de recreatie op de avifauna van het natuurmonument "de Vuntus" (Oud Loosdrecht)"

Ouderaa APM van der

Vereniging tot behoud van natuurmonumenten in Nederland
Rapport 1038

"Verkeer en recreatie in natuur en landschap"

Koninklijke Toeristenbond ANWB

Recreatiebrochure No. 17, 1976, 54 p.

"Landschapsecologische basisstudie voor het streekplangebied Veluwe 1973-1975"

Keij, P. G. en Wiegers, J.

Landbouwhogeschool Wageningen/PPD Gelderland, Arnhem
1976, 156 p.

"Eilanden onder de voet"

Werkgroep Recreatie van de Landelijke vereniging tot behoud van de Waddenzee

Vereniging tot Behoud van de Waddenzee, Harlingen, 1977, 124 p.

"Environmental Impact Report: Development of Accommodation and Facilities at Home Bay, Lake Waikaremoana"

> Urewera National Park Board, Tourist Hotel Corporation, October 1975
>
> Mr. J. Scott, Architect, for plans and drawings
> Wildlife Division, Department of Internal Affairs,
> N. Z. Oceanographic Institute, and
> Hawke's Bay Catchment Board, for data included in the Paper by Mr. P. H. W. Mylchreest.

"Mt Cook and Southern Lakes Tourist Co. Ltd: Remarkabkes Ski Field - Environmental Impact Audit"

> Commission for the Environment, 7th April, 1976
>
> This audit follows the publication of an environmental impact report on the proposed Remarkables skifield and access road, first made available in December 1975.

"Hauraki Gulf Maritime Park: Kawau Island - Working Plan"

> Prepared by: N. Z. Department of Lands and Survey for the Hauraki Gulf Maritime Park Board, November 1976
>
> This document provides the guidelines for immediate application to the management and development of the Park area on Kawau Island.

"Proposed Remarkables Ski-Field - Report on Investigations Following the Publishing of the Environmental Impact Audit on 7th April, 1976"

> Mount Cook and Southern Lakes Tourist Company Limited, 15th June, 1977
>
> A Report prepared and made available to the public by the Lands and Survey Department in conjunction with the March 1977 Lands and Survey Management Study of the Remarkables and Hector Mountains, Otago, New Zealand.

"Mt. Cook and Southern Lakes Tourist Co. Ltd : Remarkables Ski Field - Environmental Impact Audit" - "Submissions"

> Commission for the Environment.

"Remarkables and Hector Mountains, Otago, New Zealand"

A Management Study published for the Land Settlement Board by the Department of Lands and Survey, Dunedin, New Zealand, March 1977.

"Pukaki Tourist Village Planning Report"

Department of Lands and Survey, 1975.

Report dealing with the re-establishment of Pukaki Village.

SPAIN

"Tourismus und Entwicklungspolitik"

Carsten R. Moser
Veröffentlichungen des HWWA-Institut für Wirtschaftsforschung.
Hamburg. Verlag Weltarchiv GmbH. 1972, 277 p. (all.)

Nature conservation should be understood in a wider and dynamic sense, that is emphasising defense, protection and restoration. Therefore plans and programmes should systematically be preceeded by exhaustive studies on the ecological and tourist characteristics of the areas under consideration in order for the Mediterranean coastal zone (the coastline and adjacent areas), to obtain a general classification of sites with different tourism potentials.

"Tourisme et développement économique en Espagne"

Mathieu Boaglio
Paris, Documentation Française, NED N° 4048, 51 p. (Fr.)
1974

Economic impact of tourism illustrated in the case of Spain where tourism greatly contributed to the economic development of the country. An analysis of the shortcomings of Spanish tourism policy. Projections for the development of tourism demand.

"La nature et l'environnement comme infrastructure du tourisme"

Urech Manuel Aullo
Estudios Turisticos, Madrid, Numéro Spécial, Ecologia y Turismo, 36, 1972, p. 135-148.

Direct contribution of tourism to the Spanish economy (its importance for exports, balance of payments, GNP, job creation)

Tourism, as a factor of economic development (equipment building industry). Its socio-cultural impact or population structure and agriculture.

SWITZERLAND

"Tourisme et Environnement : faut-il souhaiter une concentration ou une déconcentration touristique ?"

B. Bornet, Université d'Aix-Marseille.
Centre d'Etudes du Tourisme, Aix-en-Provence
Cahiers du Tourisme, série C, N° 28, septembre 1974, 107 p. , (Fr.)

How tourism and environment are interrelated (conflicts and common aims)

Tourism and land-use planning as exemplified by Switzerland (legal measures to protect the environment, need for tourism to be spread evenly, costs of providing tourist facilities). Tourism development strategy.

"Traffic problems in holiday resorts"

Dr. Urs Schaer
AIEST (International Association of Scientific Experts in Tourism)
The Tourist Review, No. 2 April/June 1978, p. 9-15 (Engl.)

Reasons for traffic problems in holiday resorts and recreational areas. Some specific problems and their consequences for the environment.
Attempts to solve traffic problems in holiday resorts, through some examples in Switzerland.

"Tourisme et agriculture de montagne - partenaire économique naturel dans les Alpes - l'exemple de la Suisse"

Prof. Dr. C. Kaspar
AIEST (International Association of Scientific Experts in Tourism)
The Tourist Review, No. 1 January/March 1978, p. 12-14 (Fr.)

Impact of tourism on Switzerland's mountain economy, especially agriculture.
Effective measures and targets in harmonizing tourism and agriculture, the two factors in mountain region development.

"Kritische Beurteilung bisheriger methodischer Ansätze zur Bestimmung der Belastbarkeit von Erholungslandschaften. Praktisches Beispiel für die Berücksichtigung von Belastung-kriterien in der touristischen Planung"

Jost Krippendorf
AIEST (International Association of Scientific Experts in Tourism)
The Tourist Review, No. 1 January/March 1977, p. 2-7 (Ger.)

Problems of determining accommodation capacity in recreational areas.
Example showing the use of criteria for tourism planning in Switzerland.

"Probleme der Belastung und Raumplanung im Berggebiet - Problèmes de charge et d'aménagement du territoire dans les régions de montagne"

Raumplannung Schweiz, Aménagement National Suisse,
Bulletin d'Information du Délégué à l'Aménagement du Territoire, 3003 Berne, Bundesrain 20; No. 3 septembre 1978, (Fr.)

Capacity problems (ecological, economic and social) associated with mountain tourism.
The MAB programme (UNESCO) and limits of ecological capacity.
Strategies and proposals regarding the economic development of mountain regions through tourism.

"Environnement suisse : la nouvelle phase
Umwelt Schweiz: die neue Phase"

J. Stvan, J. Staub
Institut Ecoplan, Genève, 1973, 101 p. (Fr., Ger.)

Classifies events which have helped to improve environmental quality in Switzerland.
Achievements of recent ecology policy in Switzerland from a broader socio-economic standpoint.

"Regards sur le tourisme suisse"

P. Risch
Bulletin Economique et Financier de la Banque Cantonale de
Berne, No. 12, Berne, janvier 1967, 32 p. (Fr. , Ger.)

Prospects for Switzerland's tourism emerging from a review of
its role in the economy, tourist facilities (structure and use from
1950 to 1965) together with current problems. Planning and co-
ordination of measures to optimize the use of tourist amenities
while conserving them.

"Genève, les loisirs, le tourisme et l'aménagement de la ville et du
canton"

M. Baud-Bovy, N. Iten, J. P. Dellenbach, M. Rey, J. Iten,
D. C. Vitelli
Atelier Coopératif d'Architecture et d'Urbanisme,
Carouge-Genève, 1965, 54 p. (Fr.)

To avoid a reduction in Geneva's recreation areas, the ACAU
investigates sites still suitable for conservation or development
purposes, and suggests a set of programmes as the first
prerequisite for smoothly expanding Geneva's recreational
facilities.

"Fremdenverkehrsökologie, eine neue Dimension der Fremden-
verkehrslehre"

C. Kaspar
Wien, 1975, 6 p.
Festschrift von Prof. Dr. P. Bernecker p. 139-141

"Bauen als Umweltzerstörung, Alarmbilder einer Un-Architektur der
Gegenwart"

Keller Rolf
Zürich 1973

"Die formelle Umweltqualität"

Bugmann Erich
Solothurn 1975

"Probleme der Eignung und der Aufnahmekapazität touristischer
Bergregionen der Schweiz"

Bezzola A.
St. Gallen 1975

Beiträge zum Fremdenverkehr und zur Verkehrswirtschaft
herausgegeben vom Institut für Fremdenverkehr und Verkehrswirtsch
an der Hochschule St. Gallen
Bd. 7 Reihe FV

"Kapazitätsgrenzen alpiner Skigebiete"

Schönenberger Rolf L.
Zürich 1973

Inagural-Dissertation

"Les champs de ski du canton de Vaud"

Bridel Laurent
Lausanne 1970

Cahier de l'aménagement régional 10

"Gesamtkonzeption für eine schweiz. Wald- und Holzwirtschafts-
politik"

Eidg. Oberforstinspektorat
Bern 1975

"Die Berücksichtigung der ORL-Planung und des Natur- und Heimat-
schutzes bei der Konzessionierung von Luftseilbahnen"

in: ORL-Information Nr. 37/März 1975
Zürich 1975

"Le phénomène touristique et sa planification"

Bridel Laurent
Lausanne 1976

"Die bestehenden und potentiellen Skigebieten des Kanton Wallis"
Elektrowatt
Sion/Zürich 1975

"Raumplanische Eignung und Nutzungsanalysen im Berggebiet

Gresch Peter
Birmensdorf 1975

Bericht Nr. 152 der Eidg. Anstalt für forstwirtschaftl. Versuchs-
wesen Birmensdorf

TURKEY

"Tourism's Role in Economic Development: the case reexamined"

J. Diamond
Economic development and cultural change, No. 3, April 1977,
(angl.), p. 539-544

Examination of economic problems facing Turkey when promoting
tourism.

"A Decision for Touristic Investment Allocations"

Gearing, Turgut Var, Swart
AIEST (Association Internationale des Experts Scientifiques du
Tourisme)
Revue de Tourisme, No. 1, janvier-mars 1972, p. 2-13 (angl.)

An evaluation of the economic implications of tourism, taking into
account the alternative potential developments of Turkey.
Methodology.

UNITED KINGDOM

"Tourism and Development. A case study of the Commonwealth
Carribean"

John M. Bryden
Overseas Development Group, University of East Anglia.
Cambridge, at the University Press, 1973, 236 p. (angl.)

Measurement of costs and benefits of tourist development.
Discussion of tourism's social aspects and examination of the
dynamic impact of the tourist sector in the context of the smaller
islands of the Commonwealth Carribean.

"Tourism and the Economy. An Examination of Methods for Evaluating
the Contribution and Effects of Tourism in the Economy"

Gareth Richards
Department of Hotel and Catering Management
University of Hotel and Catering Management

Use of economic techniques to measure the economic impact of
tourism (direct, indirect and induced effects on output, incomes
and employment) in various sectors of the economy and:
- at an aggregative level (contribution to total national income
  and to national development),
- at a disaggregative level (contribution to individual sectors
  of the economy and to regional development).
Application of these techniques to United Kingdom and Ireland
and evaluation of the findings.

"Tourism in the Bahamas and Bermuda. Two case studies"

Brian Archer
Bangor Occasional Papers in Economics, No. 10, 1977, 96 p.
(angl.)

In addition to furnishing a detailed description of the nature of
the impact made by tourism on the economies of the two countries, the book provides a list of the general data requirements
and sources of information for studies of this type together
with a sample questionnaire and an account of the methodology.

"The Impact of Domestic Tourism"

Brian Archer
Bangor Occasional Papers in Economics, No. 2, 1973, 139 p.
(angl.)

Use of economic techniques to measure and explain the regional
implications of visitor spending and to prescribe policy measures.
Application of these techniques through a case study of the impact
of domestic tourism upon the regional economy of Anglesey,
North Wales. Examples of the impact of tourism are drawn from
many countries and from the writing of researchers in many
disciplines.

"Second Home Ownership. A Case Study"

Richard de Vane
Bangor Occasional Papers in Economics, No. 6, 111 p. (angl.)

Economic effects of second home ownership on the economy of
a rural area. Case study of the Welsh county of Gwynedd.
Examination of characteristics of second homes and their owners.
Analysis of the impact this form of tourism makes on the economy.
Details of the methodology.

"Recreation and Tourist Resources: Capacity and Measurement"

Department of the Environment, Bibliography N° 182, 1975

This list of publications is a selection of material on aspects of recreational carrying capacity defined by the Countryside Recreation Glossary (1970) as "the level of recreation use an area can sustain without an unacceptable degree of deterioration of the character and quality of the resource, or of the recreation experience"

"Tourism in Gwynedd: An Economic Study"

Institute of Economic Research, University of North Wales for Wales Tourist Board, 1974

Economic impact of tourism upon Gwynedd and evaluation of the separate contributions to the regional economy made by specific categories of tourist (defined according to the type of accommodation used).
Identification of the sectors having experienced the most benefit.

"Tourism in Appleby-in-Westmorland, Keswick and Sedbergh"

Institute of Economic Research, University of North Wales for Cumbria County Council, Cumbria Tourist Board, English Tourist Board and Lake District Special Planning Board, 1977.

Number of tourists and day-trippers who visited these 3 towns; calculation of their expenditure and evaluation of the amount of households income and employment this generated.

"The Marketing and Development of Tourism in the English Lake Counties". 1973:

"The Marketing and Development of Tourism in Northumbria". 1973
"A Study of Tourism in the North West". 1975
"A Study of Tourism in Yorkshire". 1975

by P. A. Management Consultants for the English Tourist Board.

"A Study of Tourism in the East Midlands". 2 volumes. 1976
"A Study of Tourism in East Anglia". 1976
"South East England: A Strategy for Tourism". 2 volumes. 1974

by INBUCON/AIC for the English Tourist Board.

These studies contain detailed and authoritative accounts of tourism opportunities, restraints, recommendations and policies for the region. They are based on market surveys, supply analysis, and surveys of residents and others with special interests in tourism in the region.

"Heart of England Tourism Study". 1977
"Thames and Chilterns Tourism Study". 1977

Tourism Planning and Research Ltd

These two reports, based on surveys, are designed to both contribute to the ETB's understanding and planning for tourism nationally and to aid the Regional Tourist Boards in formulating, in consultation with local authorities and others, a strategic framework for tourism planning in the region.

"A Study of Tourism in York"

English Tourist Board, 1971

The aim of this study was to provide York with a strategy for the future marketing and development of tourism in this historic city. The three main components of the study were a survey of tourists and day visitors; a survey of residents' opinions of tourism and a survey of occupancy in hotels and guest houses.

"The Holiday Industry of Devon and Cornwall"

University of Exeter for the Department of Economic Affairs and the South West Economic Planning Council. 1970

Economic effects of present and future expenditure by holiday-makers in Devon and Cornwall (particularly in relation to local incomes, industries and services).

"Tourism in Cardiganshire: An Economic Study"

University of Surrey for Wales Tourist Board, 1974

Nature and characteristics of tourism in the study area and its economic impact.
The effects of tourism expenditure on a limited but significant aspect of the general welfare or residents in the area.

"The Economic Impact of Tourism: A Case Study in Greater Tayside"

University of Edinburgh for the Scottish Tourist Board, 1975

Costs and benefits of tourism (e. g. creation of new jobs and income within a region through different types of holiday-making).
Use of regional multiplier analysis to assess the economic impact of tourism expenditure.

"Economic Survey of the Tourist Industry in the South West"

South West Economic Planning Council, 1976

This survey, which examines the tourist industry in Cornwall, Devon, most of Somerset and West Dorset, was undertaken to find the net economic benefits which the region derives from tourism as this information is a necessary starting point for future policies.

"Eastbourne Tourism Study 1976"

English Tourist Board, 1977

Surveys of tourism at Eastbourne and of its social and economic effects. Their object is to advise on the marketing and development of tourism for Eastbourne and to refine the techniques of research.

"The Economic Impact of Tourism in Edinburgh and the Lothian Region"

Roger Vaughan for the Scottish Tourist Board, 1976

The overall impact of tourism in Edinburgh and Lothian Region and the main economic benefits of tourism in terms of employment and income.

"Tourism and the Environment"

Research paper by I. Rickson, 1974. English Tourist Board (engl.)

Examination of 4 broad types of tourism:
- Recreational day tripping
- Domestic tourism
- International tourism
- Inter-continental tourism.
Definition of the "environment"; antagonistic and mutually beneficial aspects.
Major issues: overcrowding at popular sites, impact of major new developments, wear and tear on historic buildings. Role and stated objectives of the English Tourist Board.

"Tourism and the Environment"

A paper to the BTA Conference 11th November, 1971 by M. Henig. English Tourist Board, 1971 (Engl.)

Principal functions of the ETB at regional and national level, in relation to the development of tourism and the conservation of the environment.

"Planning for Tourism in England: A Planning Advisory Note"

English Tourist Board, 1978 (Engl.)

Tourism today is so important that local authorities should be able to assess its impact and opportunities and need to take it fully into account in all planning matters. The English Tourist Board in consultation with the regional tourist boards and appropriate government departments and agencies has published this advisory note for planning officers.

"A Report on Pedestrian Counts Conducted at Four Towns in the Heart of England Region"
"A Report on Pedestrian Counts Conducted at Four Towns in the Thames and Chilterns Regions"

Public Attitude Surveys Ltd. for English Tourist Board, 1977 (Engl.)

Surveys of pedestrians in towns believed to be congested at the peak of the summer season, to measure the proportions who were residents, day trippers, tourists staying in the town or elsewhere.

"Tourism in Cambridge"

City of Cambridge Planning Department, 1978 (Engl.)

Present tourist situation and possible future developments in Cambridge. Benefits and costs associated with tourism. Discussion of policies on the future role of tourism and the way in which specific problems may be dealt with in Cambridge.

"The Economic Impact of Tourist Spending in Skye"

University of Stirling for the Highlands and Islands Development Board, 1974

This study used a multiplier approach to measure the impact on income and opportunities for employment of tourist spending in Skye.

"Report on Survey of London Residents' Opinions of Tourism"

English Tourist Board, 1978

The objectives of this survey were to investigate among London residents:
1. The extent to which tourism is seen as a problem relative to other problems specific to residing in London.
2. Their impressions of the present numbers and past growth of tourists in London.
3. The advantages and disadvantages of tourism to themselves and Londoners as a whole.
4. Their own use of 'tourist' facilities.
5. Suggestions for action that might be taken by the authorities for the management of tourism.

"Survey of Eastbourne Residents Opinions of Tourism"

English Tourist Board, 1977

The objectives of this survey were to investigate amongst residents of Eastbourne Borough and 2 neighbouring parishes:
1. Impressions of the numbers of tourists visiting Eastbourne and the growth in tourism in the town.
2. The advantages and disadvantages of tourism to Eastbourne.
3. Length of residence in Eastbourne and reasons for coming to live there.
4. Usage of specified tourist facilities.
5. Usage of specified social services and amount of rates paid.

"Tourism and the Provincial Theatre in England"

English Tourist Board, 1976

A survey showing several ways in which tourism can and does benefit the provincial theatre and its patrons

"Annual Report 1976-1977"

Historic Buildings Council

A report of conservation spending on the economy of Chester.

"Annual Report 1977"

Ancient Monuments Board

A report on the wear and tear effects of visitors on Stonehenge and Silbury Hill.

"English Heritage Monitor, No. 2"

English Tourist Board, 1978

A detailed look at ancient monuments, churches and historic buildings, which appraises them from a conservation and tourism viewpoint. The main object of the Monitor is to give an annual picture of England's architectural heritage in terms of conservation, presentation, and visitor trends to assist those concerned with conservation and planning as well as those concerned with the marketing and development of tourism.

"Cathedral Tourism: A Survey of Problems and Opportunities"

English Tourist Board, 1978

The growing number of visits to cathedrals has lead to such problems as overcrowding and wear and tear on cathedral fabric. The object of the survey has been to identify pressure points and to examine means of managing tourism so as to minimize the problems arising from large numbers of visitors and to illustrate ways of increasing revenue.

"Preservation Pays: Tourism and the Economic Benefits of Conserving Historic Buildings"

SAVE Britain's Heritage

The purpose of the study is to show that Britain's historic buildings, quite apart from their intrinsic value and beauty, are a major economic resource and an irreplaceable capital asset, contributing significantly through tourism to earnings of foreign exchange, to local employment and prosperity, and to central government taxation.

UNITED STATES

"Centre de Documentation Benjamin Franklin – Environmental Bibliography"

Centre de Documentation Benjamin Franklin, Paris, September 1970, 21 p.

Under three general headings (Environment and Ecology, Pollution, and Nature Conservation) the booklet lists a series of English-language publications. The bibliography is essentially made up of short works, booklets and magazine articles from American material.

"Groupe de Recherches sur les Stratégies du Développement
Croissance et Environnement : Elements pour une Stratégie d'Harmo-
nisation"

> In "Analyse Socio-Economique de l'Environnement : Problèmes
> de Méthode", Mouton, Paris, La Haye 1973, p. 183-227,
> graphiques.
>
> Is economic growth incompatible with environmental protection,
> as so many studies claim? The article argues a different view,
> that growth itself need not be looked at askance but rather the
> forms it takes, the use made of it and the ways in which its
> fruits are distributed. A model attempts to show what happens,
> and suggests several lines of thought for conciliating economic
> development, with greater environmental protection.

"An Analysis of Environmental Quality Ranking Systems"

> FABOS Julius G.
>
> In Recreation Symposium Proceedings, USDA Forest Service,
> Northeastern Forest Experiment Station, Upper Darby, 1971,
> p. 40-55
>
> The author reviews and analyses methods of quantitative
> classification devised in North America during the 1970s, in
> order to rank environmental quality for open-air recreation.
> Twenty methods are discussed for ranking landscape quality
> and customer preferences regarding regional landscape
> features.

"Regional Recreation Land Plan: Interim Report" Detroit
Metropolitan Area Regional Planning Commission, Detroit, March
1966, 38 p.

> Rudolf B. Habben, James F. Miller and Silla G. Tomasi
>
> A study anticipating more intensive investigations, this report
> by a Detroit Metropolitan Area team reviews the natural
> resources of the region, examines the habits and aspirations of
> national and regional parks users, estimates land requirements
> for everyday recreational purposes and lays the foundations of
> regional plans (1970 and 1980) for developing existing and
> future areas.

"Proceeding from the first International Conference on the Relationship between Tourism and the Environment of Baja California Peninsula"

Feldman Arthur W. / Casco Mario et divers.

University of Southern California, Sea Grant Program, Los Angeles, 1973, 106 pages, photos.

Included in this report is the product of the efforts and the work of distinguished North Americans and Mexicans, who in this epoch of the Peninsula of Baya California, have contributed their experiences, leaving a written record of their firm willingness to achieve a development that has its objective a more meaningful evolution of the human species and human nature and not a mere mutilated development that will sadden our present vision of the future of our children.

"Factors Related to Beach Use"

Spaulding Irving

University of Rhode Island Marine Technical Report Series, Kingston, 1973, 20 pages, tables, map.

Users of relatively isolated Rhode Island beach, referred to as "Sand Beach", were interviewed on site. The author sought to determine selected characteristics of these people and the benefits they received from using Sand Beach. Factors such as solitude, involvement with the natural environment, and sensations experienced while in that natural setting could appropriately be considered in making decisions relevant to beach management.

"Modeling and Predicting Human Response to the Visual Recreation Environment"

Peterson George L. / Neumann Edward S.

In Journal of Leisure Research, Washington, Volume 1, number 3, Summer 1969, p. 219-237

Describes a strategy for measuring and analysing human visual preferences regarding the recreation environment. The aim is to develop quantitative preference functions which will take account of individual differences, and of the visual characteristics of the environment. Readily available measuring instruments (black and white photographs) and statistical methods are used; the strategy was applied for the first time to the shores of Lake Michigan in the Chicago area.

"Rhode Island's Barrier Beaches: Volume 2, Reports and Recommendations at the Community Level"

Olsen Stephen B./Grant Malcolm J.

University of Rhode Island, The Coastal Resources Center, Kingston, 1973, 114 pages, maps, tables

The report is a successor to the first volume dealing with Rhode Island's Barrier Beaches. While Volume 1 was mainly concerned with natural assets, their ecological importance and the management techniques called for in the context of action planned at the State level, Volume 2, takes the time to analyse individual beaches and suggests recommendations at the community level.

"Rhode Island's Barrier Beaches, Volume 1. A Report on a Management Problem and an Evaluation of Options"

Olsen Stephen/Grant Malcolm J.

University of Rhode Island, the Coastal Resources Center, Kingston, 1973, 118 pages, diagrams, map, plan, photograph

Part of the coastal fringe of Rhode Island comprises barrier beaches, which are narrow strips of land made up of loose materials parallel to the coast, from which they are separated by a narrow channel of water. While extremely valuable, this natural resource is unfortunately very fragile. An action and management plan to conserve it, by eliminating all types of erosion, forms the subject of part 1 of the Coastal Resources Center report.

"Trails for Indiana"

Knudson Douglas M. , Gillepsie Susan J. et al.

Purdue University, Agricultural Experiment Station, West Lafayette, Bulletin No. 1, 1973, 85 pages, diagrams, maps, photographs, annexes.

Only 1,150 of the 5,709 miles of trail in the State of Indiana are being utilized. Taking account of the needs of local and out-of-state customers, and of the extremely rich and varied natural resources, the authors put forward a full programme for the renovation and development of the trails, for a number of applications, though with the emphasis on tourism.

"Forest Recreation"

Douglass Robert W.

Pergamon Press Ltd. , Oxford, First Edition 1969, 336 pages, tables, diagrams, photographs, map

Exploitation and management of the forests in the United States must allow for fast-expanding recreational demands. This publication has the great merit of combining all problems of forest recreation planning, development and management in the light of user needs and preferences. Operators, technicians, forestry professionals, park administrators and private owners at their various levels of responsibility will find ideas, experiences and recommendations of value regarding the rational use of open spaces.

"Jalons pour l'Elaboration d'une Méthodologie de la Prospective de l'Environnement"

Barel Yves

In "Analyse Socio-Economique de l'Environnement : Problèmes de Méthode", Mouton, Paris, La Haye, 1973, p. 21-45

Environmental forecasting should address two central questions: Have we infact now reached the stage where disruption of the ecosystem as a whole or one or more local breakdown threatening the survival of man as a species are likely? If we have, or if the possibility cannot be altogether ruled out, what are the basic natural and social or else socio-natural forces which threaten with such disruption?

"Environment, Resources, Pollution and Society"

Murdoch William W. , Keyfitz Nathan et al.

Sinauer Associates Inc. , Publishers, Stamford, 1971, 440 pages, tables, graphs, diagrams, maps

Can the environment crisis be solved? One prerequisite is to understand the complex relationships between man and the land, and then translate the findings of such investigations into economic and political action. Twenty interdisciplinary experts join William Murdoch in considering ecological systems and the deteriorating environment, and suggest appropriate measures in terms of an optimum population, in balance with the natural and living environment.

"Tourism and Economic Growth: An Empirical Study"

Moheb A. Ghali, University of Hawaï.
Economic development and cultural change, No. 3, April 1976,
p. 527-5 (Engl.)

Measurement of the contribution of tourism to the growth of
Hawaï's economy: model and evaluation.

"Impact of Recreation, Vacation and Travel on New Hampshire
1954-1958-1963-1967-1970, and a Summary of the 1970 Inventory
of New Hampshire Eating and Lodging Places"

Paul Hendrick and Associates.
Office of State Planning, State of New Hampshire, Concord,
May 1971, 117 p. (Engl.)

Revises and updates research going back to 1954 in New
Hampshire, to measure the impact of tourism and open-air
recreation on the economy of the State. New Hampshire's share
of the American tourism market in 1970.

"Florida's Disney World: Promises and Problems"

L. E. Zehnder
Peninsular Publishing, 360 p., 1975 (Engl.)

Development of Walt Disney World enterprise, from its time of
inception in 1965 through ten years of growth and development.
Impact of mass tourism on Orlando's resident population and the
benefits that central Florida derived from Walt Disney World.

"Environmental Health and Human Ecologic Considerations in
Economic Development Projects"

World Bank, Washington, 142 p., 1974 (Engl.)

Primacy of the economic aspect in development, planning and
land-use projects.
The new concern for the environment, health and culture in the
quest for quality of life.

"Environmental Effects of Off-Road Vehicles: A Review of the
Literature"

N. J. Lodico
US Department of the Interior, Research Services Branch,
Office of Library Services, Washington, 112 p., 1973 (Engl.)

Reviews the major literature discussing the adverse effects of off-
road vehicles on the environment.

"Impact of Large Recreational Developments upon Semi-Primitive Environments"

J. J. Jezeski
Montana States University, Centre for Interdisciplinary Studies,
Bozeman, Research Monography No. 1, 73 p. , 1973 (Engl.)

Studies the ecological, biophysical, economic and social effects
of a project for the creation of a large-scale tourism complex
in Montana, in an area of semi-primitive plant life.

"National Shoreline Study: Shore Management Guidelines"

Center for the Environment and Man Inc.
Department of the Army, Corps of Engineers, Washington, 1972

Natural and social changes in the shoreline. A method of
rational shoreline utilization and development, in the light of
conservation and every kind of need.

"A Procedure for Evaluating Environmental Impact"

L. B. Leopold, F. E. Clarke, B. B. Hanshaw, J. R. Balsley
United States Department of the Interior, Washington, Geographical
Survey Circular 645, 13 p. , 1971 (Engl.)

How to evaluate environmental impacts so as to reconcile the
exploitation of natural resources with conservation of a pleasant
environment.

"Economic Benefits from an Improvement in Water Quality"

R. Don Shull
US Environmental Protection Agency, Office of Research and
Monitoring, Washington, 129 p. , 1973 (Engl.)

A method of evaluating the economic benefits that would accrue
from improving the quality of Upper Klamath Lake, Oregon,
whose water is polluted, as a tourist attraction. Estimates as to
how much longer tourists would stay if the quality of the water
were improved.

"The Impact of Halftracks and Airboats on the Florida Everglades Environment"

S. D. Schemnitz
Proceedings of the 1973 Snowmobile and Off-the-road Vehicle
Research Symposium, Michigan State University, Department of
Park and Recreation Resources, p. 86-117, 1974 (Engl.)

143

Environmental deterioration in the Florida Everglades due to demographic growth and the increase in tourism vehicles, particularly half-tracks and airboats.

"Estimating the Recreational and Tourist Capacity of Sensitive Mountain Recreation Areas"

L. Hamill
In "Tourism as a Factor in National and Regional Development", Trent University, Department of Geography, Peterborough, Occasional Paper 4, p. 16-24, 1975

Partial method for estimating the tourist potential of a major mountain region, the Rocky Mountains of Alberta and British Columbia. It is assumed that the long-term tourist potential equals the difference between the total recreational potential and amount of that recreational potential required by the local and regional population.

YUGOSLAVIA

"The Project on the Protection of Human Environment in the Yugoslav Adriatic Region" (The Adriatic III Project)

F. Gasparović and co-operations

Second Conference of Mediterranean Towns - Organising Committee, Rijeka, Yugoslavia, October 1976, 15 pages

Report on the course of the UNDP and the Yugoslav Government Project on the Protection of the Human Environment in the Yugoslav Adriatic Region, established in 1972. Contains summarized information on the Project, its structure and first major results.

"The Project on the Protection of the Human Environment in the Yugoslav Adriatic Region" (Final Report)

F. Gasparović and team of Project Experts and Coordinators

The Project Management, Rijeka, Yugoslavia, October 1977, 132 pages

Results of co-ordinated action of the UNDP and the Yugoslav Government Project on the Protection of the Human Environment

in the Yugoslav Adriatic Region (The Adriatic II Project) established in 1972. Contains: background information; environmental
state with scientific research results carried out in the scope of
the major environmental components such as air, water and sea
quality, land ecology, tourism, heritage, health impact, etc. ;
proposals for measures and further environmental action in the
Region.

"Tourism"

Team of experts of the Institute for the Economy of Tourism, in
charge of studies on tourism for the Project on the Protection
of the Human Environment in the Yugoslav Adriatic Region
(The Adriatic III Project)

The Yugoslav Government - UNDP Project on the Protection of
the Human Environment in the Yugoslav Adriatic Region, Rijeka,
Yugoslavia, April, 1974, 19 pages

Prepared for the First International Advisory Panel Meeting of
the Adriatic III Project, containing background information, the
state of tourist offer and demand, population issues.

"Physical Planning and Development of Tourism in the Yugoslav
Adriatic Region"

F. Gasparović and Team

The Yugoslav Government - UNDP Project on the Protection of
the Human Environment in the Yugoslav Adriatic Region, Rijeka,
Yugoslavia, March 1974, 85 pages

Study on Tourism and the Environment in the Adriatic Region of
Yugoslavia.

"Coordinating Physical Plan for the Upper Adriatic Region" (Final
Report)

Town Planning Institute of Croatia, Town Planning Institute of
Slovenia - Shankland Cox London - Otam Tourconsult Paris-
Rome (F. Gasparovic and Joint Planning Team)

Upper Adriatic Project, Rijeka, Yugoslavia, 1972, 123 pages
plus maps

Presentation of the Coordinating Physical Plan for the Upper
Adriatic Region, an area of pressures for the industrial and the
touristic development with detailed plans, maps and basic
studies.

Contains: background information, existing state, determinants and factors of development, issues of concept, population, settlements, transportation, infrastructure, conservation, etc.

"Alpine Tourist Centre Bovec" (Final Report)

Institute of Urbanism of Ljubljana - Otam Tourconsult Paris Rome (M. Debelak, G. Wolf and Joint Planning Team)

Upper Adriatic Project, Rijeka - Ljubljana, Yugoslavia, 1972, 205 pages plus maps

Presentation of the Detailed Plan for the alpine tourist centre at Bovec, Slovenia, prepared in the scope of the Upper Adriatic Project (UNDP - Yugoslavia, 1970-1972)

"KRK Island" - Strategy Plan

Town Planning Institute of Rijeka - Shankland Cox and Associates, London (A. Randić, K. Jores and Joint Planning Team)

Upper Adriatic Project, Rijeka, Yugoslavia, 213 pages including maps, June 1972

Strategy study and recommendations for future planning strategy for the island of Krk, sub-region of the largest Yugoslav port of Rijeka with pressures for both industrial and touristic develop- ment. Prepared as an additional study in the scope of the Upper Adriatic Project (UNDP - Yugoslavia, 1970-1972).

"Physical Development Plan for the South Adriatic Region of Yugoslavia - Final Report"

Town Planning Institutes of Croatia, Montenegro and Bosnia and Herzegovina (F. Gasparović and Planning Team) - Consulting Consortium Tekne, Milano - CEKOP, WARSAW (P. Radogna and Consultants)

South Adriatic Project, Dubrovnik, Yugoslavia, February 1970, 96 pages plus maps.

Regional physical development plan produced as final report of the UNDP - Yugoslavia Government Project established with the purpose of physical development planning for the coastal tourist region of the South Adriatic (1966-1969). Contains: background information, existing conditions, regional plans with population, development,transportation and conservation issues and strategy for implementation.

"Budva and Ulcinj Master Plans"
Intermediary Report: Tourism Features

The South Adriatic Project, Dubrovnik-Budva, Yugoslavia,
March 1969, 52 pages plus tables and maps

Study on sea-shore and its equipment, free time equipment, hotel
accommodation, tourist flow evolution and other considerations
and optional outlines proposed for the Master Plans for the sea
resorts of Budva and Ulcinj. Prepared in the scope of the South
Adriatic Project (UNDP-Yugoslavia, 1966-1969)

"Dubrovnik Master Plan"
and Appendices:

Vol. 1: Appendices I-V
Vol. 2: Appendices VI-XIV

Town Planning Institute of Croatia Zagreb, Institute for
Economics of Tourism Zagreb, Institute for Economics and
Planning Dubrovnik - SWECO Sweden and Associaties Denmark
(A. Marinović, C. Ivarsoon and Joint Planning Team),
January 1969, The Plan: 219 pages plus maps, Vol. 1 App.:
188 pages plus maps, Vol. 2 App.: 306 pages plus maps.

Presentation (book 1) of the Master Plan for the tourist area of
Dubrovnik with outlines for future land use concerning future
socio-economic development; Appendices (books 2 and 3) contain
geographic, urban, landscape, demographic, economic and non-
economic, housing, coastal, nautical, communicational and
other issues. Prepared in the scope of the South Adriatic Project
(UNDP-Yugoslavia, 1966-1969).

"Bilosevac - Makarska"

Detailed Plan

Town Planning Institute of Croatia Zagreb, Institute for
Economics of Tourism Zagreb - SWECO Sweden and Associates
Denmark (M. Salaj, N - F. Lenfstadins and Joint Planning Team)

The South Adriatic Project, Dubrovnik, Yugoslavia, 1969,
54 pages plus maps.

Presentation of the Detailed Plan for the Adriatic sea resort
tourist areas of Makarska and Bilosevac, prepared in the scope
of the South Adriatic Project (YNDP-Yugoslavia, 1966-1969).
Contains: background information on existing conditions,
economic determinants, town planning project, accommodation,
transportation, infrastructural, landscape and other issues.

"Split Regional Plan"

Town Planning Institute of Dalmatia Split - Shankland Cox and Associates London (B. Kalodjera, Ch. Bosel and Joint Planning Team)

The South Adriatic Project, Dubrovnik-Split, Yugoslavia, March 1970, 185 pages plus maps.

Presentation of the Regional Plan for the area of the city (port) of Split and the surrounding Adriatic communes with background information, planning strategy, implementation and recommendations. Prepared in the scope of the South Adriatic Project (UNDP-Yugoslavia, 1966-1969).

"Yougoslavie : La Côte Monténégrine"

Sauer Claude

Urbanisme, Paris, N° 129, 1972, p. 47-57, plans, cartes, photos, diagrammes.

La nécessité d'une planification intégrée du littoral monténégrin s'est concrétisée en 1967 par le lancement du "Projet Adriatique Sud". La région considérée s'entend d'une zone littorale mais aussi d'un hinterland de 100 à 150 kilomètres. Malgré de très fortes potentialités (100 à 300 000 unités d'accueil), la côte monténégrine ne sera pas entièrement livrée au tourisme de masse, puisque les deux-tiers du littoral sont protégés. Une grande diversité de formes et d'activités devrait d'autre part éviter la création de zones exclusivement touristiques ou industrielles.

OECD SALES AGENTS
DÉPOSITAIRES DES PUBLICATIONS DE L'OCDE

ARGENTINA – ARGENTINE
Carlos Hirsch S.R.L., Florida 165, 4° Piso (Galería Guemes)
1333 BUENOS-AIRES, Tel. 33-1787-2391 Y 30-7122

AUSTRALIA – AUSTRALIE
Australia & New Zealand Book Company Pty Ltd.,
23 Cross Street, (P.O.B. 459)
BROOKVALE NSW 2100   Tel. 938-2244

AUSTRIA – AUTRICHE
Gerold and Co., Graben 31, WIEN 1. Tel. 52.22.35

BELGIUM – BELGIQUE
LCLS
44 rue Otlet, B1070 BRUXELLES .Tel. 02-521 28 13

BRAZIL – BRÉSIL
Mestre Jou S.A., Rua Guaipá 518,
Caixa Postal 24090, 05089 SAO PAULO 10. Tel. 261-1920
Rua Senador Dantas 19 s/205-6, RIO DE JANEIRO GB.
Tel. 232-07. 32

CANADA
Renouf Publishing Company Limited,
2182 St. Catherine Street West,
MONTREAL, Quebec H3H 1M7 Tel. (514) 937-3519

DENMARK – DANEMARK
Munksgaards Boghandel,
Nørregade 6, 1165 KØBENHAVN K. Tel. (01) 12 85 70

FINLAND – FINLANDE
Akateeminen Kirjakauppa
Keskuskatu 1, 00100 HELSINKI 10. Tel. 65-11-22

FRANCE
Bureau des Publications de l'OCDE,
2 rue André-Pascal, 75775 PARIS CEDEX 16. Tel. (1) 524.81.67
Principal correspondant :
13602 AIX-EN-PROVENCE : Librairie de l'Université.
Tel. 26.18.08

GERMANY – ALLEMAGNE
OECD Publications and Information Centre
4 Simrockstrasse
5300 BONN   Tel. 21 60 46

GREECE – GRÈCE
Librairie Kauffmann, 28 rue du Stade,
ATHÈNES 132. Tel. 322.21.60

HONG-KONG
Government Information Services,
Sales and Publications Office, Beaconsfield House, 1st floor,
Queen's Road, Central.   Tel. 5-233191

ICELAND – ISLANDE
Snaebjörn Jónsson and Co., h.f.,
Hafnarstraeti 4 and 9, P.O.B. 1131, REYKJAVIK.
Tel. 13133/14281/11936

INDIA – INDE
Oxford Book and Stationery Co.:
NEW DELHI, Scindia House. Tel. 45896
CALCUTTA, 17 Park Street. Tel. 240832

INDONESIA – INDONÉSIE
PDIN-LIPI, P.O. Box 3065/JKT., JAKARTA, Tel. 583467

ITALY – ITALIE
Libreria Commissionaria Sansoni:
Via Lamarmora 45, 50121 FIRENZE. Tel. 579751
Via Bartolini 29, 20155 MILANO. Tel. 365083
Sub-depositari:
Editrice e Libreria Herder,
Piazza Montecitorio 120, 00 186 ROMA. Tel. 674628
Libreria Hoepli, Via Hoepli 5, 20121 MILANO. Tel. 865446
Libreria Lattes, Via Garibaldi 3, 10122 TORINO. Tel. 519274
La diffusione delle edizioni OCSE è inoltre assicurata dalle migliori
librerie nelle città più importanti.

JAPAN – JAPON
OECD Publications and Information Center
Akasaka Park Building, 2-3-4 Akasaka, Minato-ku,
TOKYO 107. Tel. 586-2016

KOREA · CORÉE
Pan Korea Book Corporation,
P.O.Box n° 101 Kwangwhamun, SÉOUL. Tel. 72-7369

LEBANON – LIBAN
Documenta Scientifica/Redico,
Edison Building, Bliss Street, P.O.Box 5641, BEIRUT.
Tel. 354429–344425

MALAYSIA – MALAISIE
and/et SINGAPORE-SINGAPOUR
University of Malaya Co-operative Bookshop Ltd.
P.O. Box 1127, Jalan Pantai Baru
KUALA LUMPUR Tel. 51425, 54058, 54361

THE NETHERLANDS – PAYS-BAS
Staatsuitgeverij
Verzendboekhandel
Chr. Plantijnstraat
'S-GRAVENHAGE   Tel. nr. 070-789911
Voor bestellingen: Tel. 070-789208

NEW ZEALAND – NOUVELLE-ZÉLANDE
The Publications Manager,
Government Printing Office,
WELLINGTON: Mulgrave Street (Private Bag),
World Trade Centre, Cubacade, Cuba Street,
Rutherford House, Lambton Quay, Tel. 737-320
AUCKLAND: Rutland Street (P.O.Box 5344), Tel. 32.919
CHRISTCHURCH: 130 Oxford Tce (Private Bag), Tel. 50.331
HAMILTON: Barton Street (P.O.Box 857), Tel. 80.103
DUNEDIN: T & G Building, Princes Street (P.O.Box 1104),
Tel. 78.294

NORWAY – NORVÈGE
J.G. TANUM A/S
P.O. Box 1177 Sentrum
Karl Johansgate 43
OSLO 1   Tel (02) 80 12 60

PAKISTAN
Mirza Book Agency, 65 Shahrah Quaid-E-Azam, LAHORE 3.
Tel. 66839

PORTUGAL
Livraria Portugal, Rua do Carmo 70-74,
1117 LISBOA CODEX.
Tel. 360582/3

SPAIN – ESPAGNE
Mundi-Prensa Libros, S.A.
Castelló 37, Apartado 1223, MADRID-1. Tel. 275.46.55
Libreria Bastinos, Pelayo, 52, BARCELONA 1. Tel. 222.06.00

SWEDEN – SUÈDE
AB CE Fritzes Kungl Hovbokhandel,
Box 16 356, S 103 27 STH, Regeringsgatan 12,
DS STOCKHOLM. Tel. 08/23 89 00

SWITZERLAND – SUISSE
Librairie Payot, 6 rue Grenus, 1211 GENÈVE 11. Tel. 022-31.89.50

TAIWAN – FORMOSE
National Book Company,
84-5 Sing Sung South Rd., Sec. 3, TAIPEI 107. Tel. 321.0698

THAILAND – THAILANDE
Suksit Siam Co., Ltd.
1715 Rama IV Rd.
Samyan, Bangkok 5
Tel. 2511630

UNITED KINGDOM – ROYAUME-UNI
H.M. Stationery Office, P.O.B. 569,
LONDON SEI 9 NH. Tel. 01-928-6977, Ext. 410 or
49 High Holborn, LONDON WC1V 6 HB (personal callers)
Branches at: EDINBURGH, BIRMINGHAM, BRISTOL,
MANCHESTER, CARDIFF, BELFAST.

UNITED STATES OF AMERICA – ÉTATS-UNIS
OECD Publications and Information Center, Suite 1207,
1750 Pennsylvania Ave., N.W. WASHINGTON, D.C. 20006.
Tel. (202)724-1857

VENEZUELA
Libreria del Este, Avda. F. Miranda 52, Edificio Galipán,
CARACAS 106. Tel. 32 23 01/33 26 04/33 24 73

YUGOSLAVIA – YOUGOSLAVIE
Jugoslovenska Knjiga, Terazije 27, P.O.B. 36, BEOGRAD.
Tel. 621-992

Les commandes provenant de pays où l'OCDE n'a pas encore désigné de dépositaire peuvent être adressées à :
OCDE, Bureau des Publications, 2 rue André-Pascal, 75775 PARIS CEDEX 16.
Orders and inquiries from countries where sales agents have not yet been appointed may be sent to:
OECD, Publications Office, 2 rue André-Pascal, 75775 PARIS CEDEX 16.

OECD PUBLICATIONS
2, rue André-Pascal, 75775 Paris Cedex 16

No. 41 409 1980
PRINTED IN FRANCE
(950 TH 97 80 03 1) ISBN 92-64-12060-2